SADDAM HUSSEIN'S GULF WARS

Map 1
Iraq and the Neighboring Countries

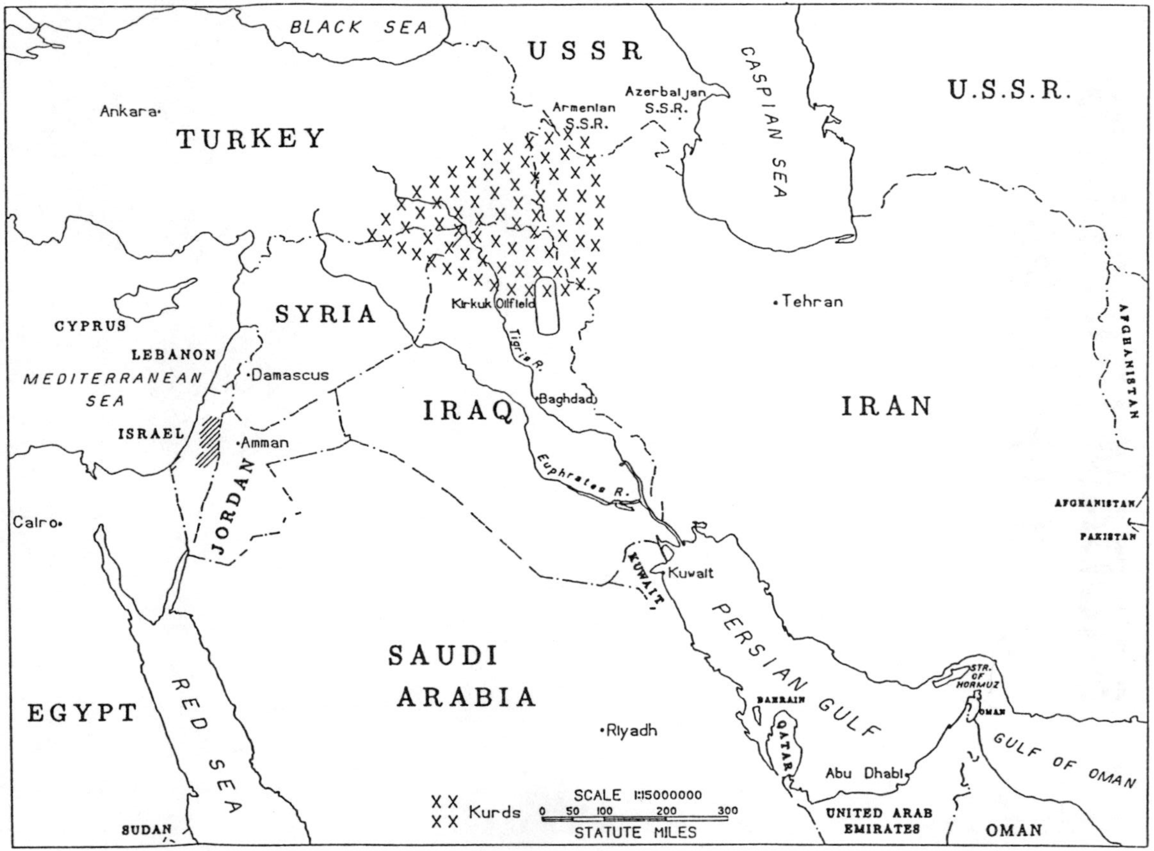

SADDAM HUSSEIN'S GULF WARS

Ambivalent Stakes in the Middle East

MIRON REZUN

PRAEGER

Westport, Connecticut
London

Library of Congress Cataloging-in-Publication Data

Rezun, Miron.
    Saddam Hussein's gulf wars : ambivalent stakes in the Middle East
/ Miron Rezun.
        p.   cm.
    Includes bibliographical references and index.
    ISBN 0-275-94324-0 (alk. paper)
    1. Iraq—Politics and government.   2. Hussein, Saddam, 1937-
3. United States—Foreign relations—Iraq.   4. Iraq—Foreign
relations—United States.   I. Title.
DS79.7.R49   1992
956.704'3'092—dc20   92-4197

British Library Cataloguing in Publication Data is available.

Library of Congress Catalog Card Number: 92-4197
ISBN: 0-275-94324-0

First published in 1992

Praeger Publishers, 88 Post Road West, Westport, CT 06881
An imprint of Greenwood Publishing Group, Inc.

Printed in the United States of America

The paper used in this book complies with the
Permanent Paper Standard issued by the National
Information Standards Organization (Z39.48-1984).

10 9 8 7 6 5 4 3 2 1

This book is dedicated to all the innocent children of the Middle East who have suffered and died from the madness of war.

Contents

Preface and Acknowledgments

The U.S. secretary of state, James Baker, the most committed person in the entire American government to deal-making and to political settlements in the volatile Middle East, actually played a far weaker role in the events of the Gulf conflict than President George Bush. Harmony between the White House and the U.S. State Department in framing foreign policy was not always apparent. In this last war against Saddam Hussein, it was not expected to be. Nor did it matter in the end. For the result of that last war was an opportunity gained by the United States and an opportunity lost by Iraq's Saddam Hussein. Both countries had valuable stakes to fight for.

When the war ended, political analysts wanted to explain it; historians were seeking reasons why it began. Mideast leaders were anxious to capitalize on it, and U.S. war heroes were prepared to write their reminiscences about it.

Less than a year after the liberation of Kuwait from the Iraqi stranglehold, an international Mideast peace conference opened in Madrid-- this time largely the fruit of James Baker's peace shuttles to the Arab capitals and to Israel. The conference aim was to discuss the many insurmountable problems of the Arab-Israeli conflict, at the core of which lay the Palestinian issue. The very fact that the conference could be held was in itself one of the aftereffects of the two Gulf wars. It is sad for the world, I must say, that neither Iran nor Iraq was at this time involved in the peace deliberations. These two Gulf powers have remained on the sidelines, opposed to any peace settlement and committed to supporting the hard-line segment of the Arab populations.

This particular development, in addition to the revelation about General Norman Schwarzkopf's contract with Bantam Books for a definitive memoir on the war, impelled me to write my own evaluation of the Mideast situation, focusing primarily on the Gulf wars and on the policies of Iraq and the United States. In earlier publications, I made ample references to the way the United States saved Saddam Hussein from the onslaught of Khomeini's Iran.[1]

I return to this theme again; this time, in far greater detail, I explain why this was so and how the White House and the Pentagon ultimately resolved to go to war against Saddam Hussein while a settlement was still pending. The two main imperatives of U.S. Mideast policy ultimately were to cripple Saddam Hussein's war machine for good and to resurrect in the American people that confidence and that pride they once had in the nation as a world leader, a world peacemaker, a post-Gulf War plus post-Cold War healer.

The stakes in the Middle East will remain extremely complex. The very semantics of the region, the social and ethnic forces at play here, the economic and historical disparities are all so different that real peace in the Middle East, in our lifetime, may prove to be illusory. The Soviet Union as we knew it no longer exists. The United States, too, is passing through a period of relative economic decline. But, in the Middle East, the U.S. is still regarded as the only country capable of spearheading a movement toward lasting peace. Will the American leaders prove equal to the task of peacemaking in the same way as they have proven they could gain opportunities and influence from the success of an armed conflict? The memoirs of an American general will not tell us the whole truth. Historians will for many years ponder over the moot questions of the Gulf War and America's involvement in it.

Under no circumstances should the reader treat this book as anything more than a fairly recent analysis of events. Far from exhaustive, this is not a concise history. It is meant for the general reader as well as the expert academic; it is a tight redefinition, a hindsight reevaluation and, I hope, it will not stand as a biased view. However, the reader who thinks that I am not going to engage in *ad hominem* polemics will be gravely disappointed.

I wish to extend a sincere thanks to my assistant, Angela Williams, for helping me research the heady events of 1990 and 1991. I also wish to thank Marc Milner, the coordinator of the Military and Strategic Studies Program at the University of New Brunswick, for offering me generous financial assistance, and to Joyce Agnew of the Canadian Department of National Defense, for additional funding that enabled me to make trips to the Middle East. The funds were necessary to conduct interviews, and to cover the cost of finalizing a manuscript that went through several drafts. Barbara Wild and Alda Trabucchi did an excellent job with copy-editing. But it was Dan Eades of Praeger Publishers in New York who had to bear with my idiosyncracies, though he repeatedly told me that he knows good things when he reads them, and it was he who decided to bring this book to the world as quickly as possible-- while interest in the Middle East is at its peak.

Note

1. See my two books: *Post-Khomeini Iran and the New Gulf War* (Quebec: Centre Québécois des Relations Internationales, 1991) and *Intrigue and War in Southwest Asia: The Struggle for Supremacy from Central Asia to Iraq* (New York: Praeger, 1992).

Prologue

It was August 2, 1990. I was sitting in the shade of a poplar, on the multi-colored patio of Geneva's famous *cité universitaire*, when the quiet of the soft morning breeze was rudely disturbed by a news bulletin. The voice on the French-language radio station announced that Iraqi forces had but a few hours before crossed the border of Kuwait. The summer guests looked dumbfounded. An atmosphere of mixed confusion and bewilderment hung heavy in the air.

Geneva was my favorite summer haunt in Europe. I had studied at its university more than a decade ago. Now and again I would come back to meet with old friends, exchange notes, and continue my research on international affairs. On this day a group of *Maghrebins* (North African Arabs from Algeria) invited me to sit down to tea with them.

On our hearing the news, a grim, death-like silence cleaved the air. One of my Algerian friends stood up, raised his thin glass of tea skyward, blurted something in a gloating manner, and quickly announced that it was high time the valiant soldiers of Saddam Hussein were beginning the long-expected unification of all the Arabs. His hatred of the West was at flashpoint. He expressed a disdain for the rich Arabs of the Gulf. He was visibly moved and proud of what had happened. Yet he was a North African, so conscious of his French heritage. Without any hesitation, he broke into his familiar Algerian dialect. He paused for a moment. His next comment was genuine praise for Allah.

Taking a cue from him, the other Algerians quickly agreed. Our Swiss onlookers, milling about, wanted no part of our conversation. The Algerians had a reputation for loudness; their naturally aggressive streak only frightened the slow and ponderous Swiss, who, in any case, never failed to show a subtle contempt for dark-skinned foreigners. But the *Maghrebins* could easily speak to me. I was, after all, a Middle Easterner, too. That day

I could only feel indignation at the turn of events in the Gulf region. I didn't care if Saddam wanted to run away with Kuwait. But I told them that Saddam was a megalomaniac and a political gambler. The conversation abruptly ended on that note.

Saddam Hussein and his Iraqi regime had soon annexed Kuwait. Saddam Hussein had overtly challenged the West. He was calling and preparing for the final showdown with the American-led forces in nothing less than the grandiloquent terms of "the mother of all battles." In the months that followed I spent a great deal of time watching the unfolding drama on CNN (Cable News Network beaming from Atlanta, Georgia) and reading whatever snippets of news I could find. A number of incidents during and after the war impelled me to take more than a passive interest in these developments. The most startling of all, I discovered, was the element of allegory and symbolism in the dramatically unfolding events, the constant references to destiny, God, and the pursuit of human struggle and fulfillment. The Arabs used to recite such allegories in heroic songs.

In the popular lore of folktales passed down from generation to generation by Arab storytellers there is one particular tale that stands out above all the rest. Like all epic tales, rhythmic, onomatopoeic, true to the genius of literary metaphors, it comes replete with flamboyant images of war and glory. It is a masterpiece of oral narration in Arabic, probably spun out by successive poets and bards, each one adding a bit more to the story. There is something markedly symbolic, even prophetic, about its substance. It is rich in truths and half-truths, and, to the Western ear, it is strangely reminiscent of predictions made by the European sage, Nostradamus. The first such prophecy came from the twelfth-century poet, Mohi Aldin bin Arabi.

It goes something like this:

> The forces of the Franks [which may easily mean the Westerners--Europeans and Americans, etc.] and the Egyptians will one day all perish in battle; ... [they will be] utterly defeated in the desert by a man named Saddam.

Then the prophecy accelerates the cadences with apocalyptic, hauntingly life-like pronouncements:

> When the Jews [meaning Israelis] are united with the crusaders [i.e., the West] and fly on iron horses [aircraft],
>   When the Aqsa Mosque [which is located in the city of Jerusalem and is one of Islam's holiest places] is taken prisoner,
>   When rule is in the hands of women [i.e., former prime ministers Margaret Thatcher of Great Britain, Benazir Bhutto of Pakistan, and Golda Meir of Israel],

When fire emerges in the Gulf and rule in the Hejaz [the coastal area of Saudi Arabia where Mecca and Medina are located] falls into the hands of perverse people,
And people capable of waging war in the stars come to their capitals
And oil flows into the Gulf
And the yellow races come from the East, who call for oceans
      of blood to cover the area
Then the one-eyed charlatan will appear.

Obviously the Israelis and the West are united against Iraq and they fly in planes. To Muslim eyes, the Aqsa Mosque in Jerusalem is a prisoner of the Jewish state. Women have ruled a number of different countries, including Muslim Pakistan. The Gulf has seen gunfire and could have been set on fire from oil tanks and the refineries that ramify the Gulf coast. The Hejaz in the hands of perverse people could be said to symbolize the Americans and other Western allies in the holy places of Saudi Arabia. And who could possibly deny that Americans and Russians are capable of waging war in outer space? These prophecies would be fulfilled, but not before the coming of a false prophet. Was the false prophet supposed to have been the Ayatollah Khomeini? Could it be U.S. president George Bush? Perhaps former Soviet president Mikhail Gorbachev? Surely it could not be his rival, the blustering Boris Yeltsin?

There is another chilling prophecy about a man named Sadim from Babel. The reader will note that Babel is the capital of old Babylon, where Iraq is now situated. Sadim was supposed to use a fire to destroy an army of Jews, Christians, Turks, and Egyptians. If there is to be a false prophet, then there must also be a redeemer. Sadim from Babel would fit the description of a redeemer. This could be taken to mean that he is Saddam Hussein. The fire could be interpreted as being a nuclear bomb.

Saddam's war against the West--some will say it was a defense against the West--only lasted six weeks. No chemical weapons were used. No one released a nuclear device. The hostilities ended by the first week of March 1991. Around that time the Kurds began another uprising in northeastern Iraq and took over the town of Mosul. But within a week, the Kurdish rebels were routed and the whole Kurdish population was put to flight into the mountain havens of northern Iraq, Iran, and Turkey. The tragedy of the Kurds was heartrending to behold. Their exodus from Iraq began reaching Biblical proportions. Two and a half million people were on the run, haggard, demoralized, stung by rain, buffeted by fierce mountain winds, and chilled to the bone by the nighttime cold. They had little or nothing to eat, only melted snow to drink, a few blankets to keep themselves warm. Their infants died in droves. These people felt betrayed and abandoned by the West. It was not the first time it happened. Yet Saddam, paradoxically, survived it all.

The following week, in the house of a friend who was a pious man of Indian descent, I sat admiring a striking painting of the Vedic god Krishna sitting in a chariot with the warrior Arjuna. They were preparing for a battle against an opposing army of kith and kin. The enemies were brothers and cousins, arrayed like phalanxes, on the mythical field of Kuruksetra. Krishna was going to help Arjuna and his soldiers win the battle. Krishna was all-powerful, and the armies of the enemy host were about to be destroyed. Krishna had decided which side it was wise for him to take. There would always be a right side and a morally wrong side. Krishna would decide.

I asked my Indian friend if Krishna, who was depicted in the painting as a beautiful young boy, had any remorse? Why did Krishna take sides? Who could Krishna be? He answered that Krishna was "the power that is." This Vedic god was the ultimate arbiter and the ultimate redeemer. In modern terminology, my friend hinted, it could be someone like President Bush. It is any force or power that can decide the fate of mere mortals and the outcome of events.

What happened subsequently was that I received an invitation to go to Turkey from Professor Ali Fuat Borovali of Bilkent University in Ankara. The Turks had now begun speaking freely about the Kurds and were trying to help them as best they could. Borovali suggested that I come and see for myself the plight of the Kurdish children on the border. I knew that wherever the Kurds had settled, wherever they lived, like gypsies, they were usually despised by Turks, Iranians, and Iraqis alike. American decision-makers also had developed a clear-cut policy on the Kurds, which was not particularly to my liking, although I realized the sensitive position the U.S. government was in.

Nor were these people well served by their own leaders. They seemed to be in the same predicament as the Palestinians, but the Palestinians at least have had very strong support from the Arabs as a whole. It seemed to me that God had abandoned the Kurds. Either that or President Bush had left them in the lurch. Pressured by other world leaders, moved by a public outcry, Bush eventually did help them. But it was all too little, too late.

In the lifetime of a nation and in the lives of men and women who go through periods of upheaval, the occurrence of war occupies a central place. There are so many events that precede it, so much that accompanies it, so much that follows after. War often appears as the grisly catalyst in human destiny. The political fortunes of world leaders frequently depend on it. Since recorded history--from ancient China to the present day--much has been written about it. The commonly debated questions are: What morality can there possibly be in war? Is war necessary and just, whatever the circumstances, whatever the conditions? Why must human beings go through it? Can anything be learned from it? Whether it be good or bad, war, in short, is about differences between peoples and cultures; it is about envy and pride, jealousy and hate.

What immediately leaps to the eye is that war continues the sad story of politics and power. It is also said that politics and power are one and the same thing. And, of course, resorting to war must be the only appropriate way to end the problems of conflicting power relationships. The prominent nineteenth-century German scholar/soldier/strategist Karl von Clausewitz once ruminated about the semantics of war with words to that effect.

In his epic *War and Peace* (1869), the Russian novelist Leo Tolstoy pursued the theme of war from a philosophical point of view. He spoke directly to his readers about the greatness and evil in men when tested beyond their capacities. Much about the personality and the character of nations emerges in time of war. Tolstoy said that during war there is also much that can be learned about human frailty. He thought that Napoleon Bonaparte, for instance, the man who ravaged Europe in his day and who dared to invade Russia in 1812, would in time turn out to be little more than a paltry figure in European history. Napoleon, to be sure, was not so insignificant. Neither was he as evil and vile as he was made out to be. But to Tolstoy this did not matter. Napoleon was an upstart, had caused a major war, and any war, Tolstoy argued, was the "vilest act yet devised by man;" cruel, callous and amoral.

The French emperor, we already know in hindsight, paled in comparison with subsequent warmongers. Far more wicked men were destined to outperform him in sheer villainy. History reminds us how Hitler, for instance, came to power in Germany, how he ended up taking his own life after causing a war that swept away the lives of millions.

Since Hitler's total bloodletting, there have been wars galore: small wars, colonial wars, liberation wars, just wars, cold wars, hot wars, twilight wars, wars by proxy. But nothing since the Korean War of the early 1950s has so captured the attention of the world public as Saddam's wars. Saddam first went to war against Iraqi Kurds; he then fought against Iran. Next he invaded his fellow Arabs in Kuwait, and the final showdown came when a U.N.-sponsored and U.S.-led coalition of Arab and Western states was sent against him.

By the time it came to this last confrontation, the whole Gulf War became packaged in a new communication medium: "*television.*" People in the West who had always despised such vile undertakings suddenly began to curse the whole thing, no less because their favorite television show had been preempted, nay, invaded, by war coverage. The "television war," unrivaled by any other war in this century, including Vietnam, overloaded the senses with vivid scenes: Allied field commanders, with their braggadocio, in desert fatigues; Israeli children wearing gas masks and huddling in anterooms against the bosoms of their parents; Arab street mobs calling for American deaths; a larger-than-life American commanding general; a "kick-ass" president of the United States arrogantly trumpeting battle successes; over four million attending a ticker-tape victory parade down Wall Street in the heart of New York City. Viewers and listeners were exposed almost daily to what the media decided was nothing less than a madman--the Iraqi leader, Saddam Hussein. We all became armchair participants in that war.

In his classic study of the American government bureaucracy and of the office of the U.S. Presidency, Hedrick Smith, a prolific American *New York Times* journalist, relates how the media like to mislead and exaggerate. He points to the Americans' tendency "to reduce the intricacy of a hundred power plays to the simple equation of whether the president is up or down, winning or losing on any given day or week. Television and the viewing millions seek to make a simple narrative of complex events. Television news feeds the public appetite to treat events as binary--good or bad, up or down, progress or setback, winners or losers--and to push aside more complex layers of reality."[1]

Nor did the media fail in its unstinting devotion to manipulating the Arab image. It was done to bolster the image of Western soldiers and Western leaders. Misrepresentation of Arabs and their Islamic faith had always gone unchallenged in Western popular culture. And the Western psyche was only too happy to nurture a bias against practically all Arabs. Edward Said, professor of English literature at Columbia University, said in his book *Orientalism*, "The life of an Arab Palestinian in the West, particularly in America, is disheartening."

Students of the Arab world and of Islamic affairs readily believe that T. E. Lawrence of *Seven Pillars of Wisdom* fame had a penchant for things Arabic. The only thing that Lawrence liked about the Arabs was Arab boys. His *Seven Pillars of Wisdom* is in fact sprinkled with unflattering comments about the Arab people. In much the same way, Karl Marx, a German racist, but a remarkable social critic, made constant remarks about the "trash of nations" (*Gesindel der Nationen*), in reference to the South Slavic "riff-raff," and even berating the Russian masses themselves. This was peculiar to most German intellectuals of the time, particularly common among left-leaning and right-leaning German Hegelians.

There is, of course, nothing strange in the way Westerners generally feel about the Arabs today: Arab men are thought to lust after money, power, and Western women. Arab women are often portrayed as giggling harem girls or belly dancers. Most Western movies about Arabs rely upon swords, camels, and tents as the ubiquitous props.

Raiders of the Lost Ark (1981), one of the biggest box-office hits of all time (with Harrison Ford as the intrepid Indiana Jones), featured many such examples of East versus West. In one scene, a menacing black-robed swordsman challenges the American hero to mortal combat. But

Indiana, with a gleam of contempt in his eye, shows no fear, only a laconic boredom. While the Arab displays a dexterous proficiency with a scimitar, the American, confident of superior technological prowess, quietly slips his hand into a holster, draws his gun, and shoots his Arab adversary dead. Movie audiences clap and find the whole sequence uproarious. The only good Arab in the entire film is Indiana's sycophantic sidekick--Sallah. This MGM production was later criticized as overly condescending toward Arabs and called one of the most controversial motion pictures ever made.

Contemporary Arab nations and societies have for years been sub-jected to the same distortions, underlying an over-simplification in Western ethnic assumptions. From television to film to newspapers to rock music, Arabs are all too often portrayed as murderous thugs. Kuwaitis and Saudis are depicted as ostentatiously wealthy and too lazy or cowardly to fight their own battles; Iraqis are psychopaths who torture and maim; Palestinians are desperate fanatics who espouse terrorism. The Western public mind believes that Arabs are violent, lascivious, fanatical, avaricious, and congenitally stupid. It is an attractive stereotype; it skillfully plays on emotions and fantasies. It casts all logic and reason to the winds.

Take, for instance, the fact that Arab sheikhs were prominent villains in a score of Hollywood movies. Imagine the macho Rudolph Valentino leaping across the sands in a 1920s Hollywood melodrama--with the hot *hamsin* (sandstorm) blowing--to snatch the hapless fair-haired Western woman to his horse. He abducts and seduces her in that proverbial tent somewhere in a remote corner of the windswept wilderness. For a moment one wonders whether the ravished woman is truly his victim. When the seduction is complete, we stand in awe of a powerful Arab phallocrat, now touted for all to see as the perfect male sex symbol. Consider the market-ability of it all when North America puts out a line of condoms that is sold under the trade name "Sheik". In 1991, after the American victory in the Gulf War, a new condom appeared on the market, aptly called "Desert Shield"--to give American machismo a little boost at this time.

The images are all distortions. They are filtered by our own stereo-types, refracted by a media anxious to entertain the gullible public or to serve the political leadership. Quite the contrary to the stereotype, the Arabs are in fact the very people who perfected writing, medicine, and other sciences while Europe was culturally still in the Dark Ages. The rich traditions of the various Arab, and Islamic-based, empires provided us with our numerical system and a basis for architectural design and astronomy. They codified a system of Islamic law that became universal for mankind. Here is a people who once captured Jerusalem, who added to and never desecrated the spiritual value of that Holy City. They then defended it against the savage attacks of coarse Crusaders. The Arabic-Persian culture of Baghdad, which flourished under the Abbasid Empire during the eighth and ninth centuries, cultivated poetry, philosophy, mathematics, law,

Koranic studies, science, medicine, astronomy, and history. When it comes to storytelling can there be any greater pleasure than reading *The Thousand and One Nights*, a literary Arabesque narrated by an enchanting Scheherazade? She fires our imagination with tales of (there were really a thousand in all) Ali Baba, Sinbad, and Aladdin and his magic lamp. A people such as this ought to be remembered for their contributions to Western civilization in these fields. Yet what we have here is a people treated with contempt and derision.

The negative image of Arabs has been bolstered by the personality and actions of Saddam Hussein. And why is it that we take such satisfaction in vilifying this Iraqi leader? Was he not close to the hearts of most Arabs, so dear even to non-Arab Muslims, from the far-flung reaches of Indonesia to the Muslim periphery of the former Soviet Union? Arab North Africans admired him. Arab Palestinians absolutely revered him. His star rose and faded with the fortunes of his military glories. Once at the pinnacle of power in the Arab world, he was, in defeat, reduced to struggling for his personal power inside Iraq. The ignominy of failure came in the wake of Saddam's wanton destruction of the Gulf's ecology. Saddam ruined the lives of hundreds of thousands of Iraqi Kurds, he desecrated Shi'a holy places, devastated the Kuwaiti infrastructure, wasted the lives of young Iraqi soldiers, and dangerously challenged the might of Israeli arms. In the end, Saddam lost the war against the West.

What would be the purpose of demonizing this man without giving an account of what has made him a demon? Saddam, after all, is as much a product of the Arab nation as Hitler was of the German. Now Saddam has been cast in the role of the archetypal evil Arab. Journalists and commentators, taking a cue from U.S. president George Bush, repeated at every turn how Saddam's calculations resembled Hitler's. Small wonder that after Saddam's defeat he became subjected to the same vilification as the Führer of the Third Reich.

The struggle of Saddam Hussein is the struggle of a man who typifies the Arab Mideastern mind-set. His actions explain to what extent the majority of Arabs have fallen out with what they perceive as Western, and particularly American, domination of a region over which Arabs once ruled supreme. His policies also attest to an inner Arab desire for unity under the banner of Arab nationalism, spearheaded and exemplified by the Iraqi republic.

We will never comprehend the politics of Iraq, nor will we understand Saddam Hussein's motives, unless we understand the Arabs as a people, the Muslim component of their character, and the role the West plays in this region. As renowned international journalists Pierre Salinger and Eric Laurent revealed in their *Secret Dossier: The Hidden Agenda Behind the Gulf War*, "The Americans did not understand Saddam Hussein or his mentality, and Saddam Hussein did not understand the United States and its mentality."[2]

The personality of Saddam Hussein is truly baffling. His policies are bewildering. His demeanor is perhaps less perplexing to the Arabs and to the Muslims of all nations; we can't say his behavior would elicit much surprise among Third World peoples. Hitler was unilinear; Saddam has been foxier. He has in him both the cunning artful dodger and the plunderer. Alternately, he is a militant secularist and a pious Muslim; a socialist, a nationalist, and a free-marketeer; a strong Iraqi and an equally strong pan-Arabist; the scourge of the West and the pragmatic statesman of the "status quo," a man the West could safely rely on. In effect Saddam has been chameleon-like, metaphoric, in both word and deed. Like an ambitious modernizer, he wanted to move quickly, to relive the glories of the Arab and pre-Islamic past. He was willing to gamble for the highest stakes possible. It did not matter much and he could care much less if his enterprise was headed for disaster.

For over a decade Iraq has been a major player in world affairs. The pages that follow are essentially an explanation of the distorting double mirrors of Saddam Hussein's politics, the politics that ultimately dragged his country, the Persian Gulf region, and the West to war. The story continues to explain how the West made its biggest mistakes about Saddam Hussein's regime and why.

The picture we have in the second half of this book of a mighty Iraq with its million-man army invading puny Kuwait is also a distortion. Many factors are at play in this drama, many more than the usual stakes of oil and nationalism. The will to war in this episode is intimately bound up with historical error, greed, individual charisma, poverty, fear, and the ambivalence of the West's relationship with the whole Middle East.

NOTES

1. Hedrick Smith, *The Power Game: How Washington Works* (New York: Ballantine Books, 1988), p. 10.

2. Pierre Salinger and Eric Laurent, *Secret Dossier: The Hidden Agenda Behind the Gulf War*, trans. from the French by Howard Curtis (New York: Penguin, 1991), p. viii.

SADDAM HUSSEIN'S
GULF WARS

**Map 2
Iraqi Refugees, April 19, 1991**

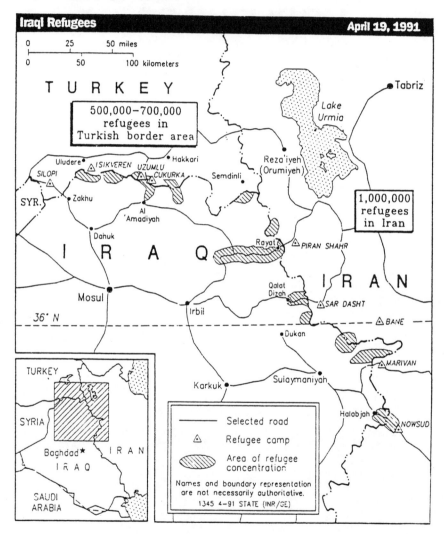

The Arabs, Islam, and the West

People in the West have by and large ignored the differences between Judeo-Christian and Arab-Islamic ideals. The Western public, with its own social mores and culture, tends to superimpose a Western morality on the unpredictable environment of the Middle East. The result is that Westerners usually end up judging Middle Easterners too harshly. The reason for this is that Western logic often follows a narrow rationality and has difficulties trying to make out the complexities of Arab thought patterns. This Western rationality then turns irrational itself when, failing to comprehend the East, the Arabs, and the Muslims, it becomes unduly biased and prejudiced against them.

Western morality has been simplified to extremes by Cartesian thinking as well as by a rationality born of the Protestant work ethic and the empirical methods of science. This imposed a narrow rationality which insists that the human species can only function in such a way. But any quest for a calculable rationality in human affairs in the end defies the incalculable subjectivity of human beings.

In the Mideast context, Arab-Islamic rationality and life and death struggles are ultimately bound up with Allah, or God. But this too is narrowly rational, and even irrational, for it rests on the assumption that everything, indeed all human actions, is predestined by Allah. Certainly Judaism and Christianity have modified the development of this deterministic view of man and have conceded that the universe does not run a predestined course. Yet the Arab is all too familiar with the expression *Insh' Allah!* (God willing!) Predestination and fatalism are still strongly anchored in the Arab mind, whether it be the future of a single individual or of an entire nation.

All Muslims, whether they are Iranic (Pushtuns, Baluchi, Persians,

Kurds), Turkic (Azeris, Turks, Uzbeks, Tatars), or Arabs (Shi'a and Sunni), divide the world into two parts: "*dar al-Islam*" (the world of Islam) and "*dar al-harb*" (the world of war). The *dar al-Islam* includes the Muslim world; it also includes the adherents to other religions Muslims would like to but do not always, tolerate such as the Christians and Jews, the "People of the Book." The *dar al-harb* includes the world of the infidels, or unbelievers who have had no prophets, those peoples and nations with neither a Moses nor Jesus nor a commandment nor holy book (Bible, Koran, etc.) to live by. Yet Muslims often feel impelled--and this has been an incongruity about Christianity as well--to declare a jihad upon Christian Westerners, or anyone else they regard as hostile "infidels." Jihad, or holy war, was thus inculcated in the Arab mind and carries with it purely political overtones.

True enough, at the outset Islam held that all war, except holy war, was to be forbidden! Jihad did not always imply a violent war, but a simple, peaceful conversion to Islam. But no one in Islam ever elaborated on what constituted "holy war," and this concept became blurred. Iran's Khomeini used it to justify his struggle against the West and against Saddam Hussein. Khomeini used the term in relation to Israel as well. Saddam Hussein used it to couch his standoff against the Allied coalition forces behind a more convincing religious rhetoric.

Why be surprised over such paradoxes and double standards? For centuries Christianity was itself characterized by religious jealousy, an intolerance, and a belief that Christian ethics and the tenets of Jesus (ideas that were never repudiated by Muslims) were the only true and valid ones. Christianity held that all other faiths were in error. The Christian Church, moreover, imposed its faith, by force if necessary, on all unbelievers, including pious Muslims. Pope Urban II, who launched the First Crusade to liberate the Holy Land from the Muslims, said it was a divine mission to fight against that "race which is foreign to God."

Arabs understand the language of holy war, especially if it is pronounced against foreigners. It derives from the self-perpetuating Arab-Muslim doctrine of *Din Muhammad bi'l-sayf* ("the religion of Mohammed with the sword"), requiring Muslims to spread the faith by force of arms. Nor is the Arab component lacking here. For Mohammed was himself the first truly Arab general, the first Arab conqueror. Over time, the Arabs fostered the belief that it was primarily the Islamic faith that in centuries past enabled them to achieve cultural and military superiority over the West. When Arab-Islamic power waned, the Turks emerged as the dominant power in the Middle East. The Ottomans were nonetheless regarded by all Arabs as Muslims. Though held in contempt, Turkish culture was still regarded by the Arabs as an extension of Islam, its mailed fist, as it were. Likewise, the origins of Saladin, who beat the Western Crusaders, are also blurred--for Saladin was really a Kurd, not an Arab. I shall come back to this point later on.

Arabs might feel about Saladin whatever they wish, but the Islamic world is, politically speaking, far from being homogeneous. History will explain this best. Soon after Mohammed's death, a split occurred within Islam, and this split has divided the Muslims ever since. Generally Muslims split into Sunni (the majority, denoting the "right path") and the Shi'a.

How did this come about? When he died, Mohammed left no direct male heirs, causing a power struggle among his followers. Many felt that Ali ibn 'Abi Taleb, Mohammed's cousin and son-in-law, his faithful aide and champion warrior, who had been the first convert to Islam, ought to become the Prophet's successor. Ali's supporters argued that when Mohammed first asked his relatives to accept Islam, he promised that the first to do so would become his successor. According to tradition, they were all confused. Ali was the only one who did not hesitate. For this, Mohammed apparently declared him successor and vice-regent.

However, after Mohammed's death, Abu Bakr (father of the Prophet's favorite wife, Aisha) became the leader, and eventually 'Umar ibn Khattab (Abu Bakr's supporter and father of Hafsa, another of the Prophet's wives) took over, though he proved to be unsuited for the role. When he died, there were two possible successors: Ali and Othman. Ali was at a disadvantage since he was opposed by Aisha and Mu'awiya ibn Abi Sufian (brother-in-law of the Prophet). Othman (of the Ummayad clan) was thus chosen but was soon assassinated. Finally it was Ali's turn to become the fourth caliph or successor. But Ali was assassinated during the month of Ramadan (A.H. 40). Those who supported Ali became known as the *Shi'at Ali* (or Partisans of Ali), or simply Shi'ites.

Shi'ism thus became a form of dissent among revolutionary elements. Ali's death forms the key martyrdom for the Shi'a sect of Islam. After Ali's death, Mu'awiya ibn Abi Sufian became caliph. Soon afterward, Mu-had Hasan (Ali's elder son) was poisoned and Mu'awiya's son, Yazid, was made heir. When Yazid came to power, he had his own men kill Hussein (Ali's other son) and his three sons in the battle of Karbala. All of Hussein's companions were killed except his son Zain al Abidin and Zain's son Mohammed al Baqir. The upshot of all this is straightforward. First, these episodes all took place in present-day Iraq, at Najaf and Karbala. Iranians espoused Shi'ism, including the Arabs of southern Iraq. These divisions must be understood. They must have been important enough for Ayatollah Khomeini to constantly refer to Saddam Hussein as Yazid during the Iran-Iraq war.

The modern Iraqi state may be divided into three distinct components. The Shi'a Arabs live in the southern parts, in the general region of Iraq's second largest city, Basra. They account for approximately 60 percent of the entire population. On the religious plane, their affinity would seem to lie with the Iranian Shi'ites. The Sunni Arabs and the Sunni Kurds (who follow mainstream Islam) constitute the remainder of the Iraqi population.

But the fragmentation of Iraq does not stop there. The Arabs were historically separated by tribe-like sects, clans, and villages. The allegiance of the people is, first and foremost, accorded to the leaders of the tribe, the sect, or the village. In pre-Islamic Arab society the people were primarily tribal nomads or Bedouins. It would take a considerable length of time for Arab society to rid itself of the tribal mentality, although, on the surface, it is definitely achieving this. Helping it are the inexorable processes of Islamization and Arabization, which go hand in hand and have become part of an Arab/Muslim mythology.

Islam itself has always tended toward empire building. The tribal features of the Arab Muslims are really pre-Islamic traits, as are many features of Christianity either pagan or heritages of pre-Christian times. In pre-Islamic times, the Arabs were idolatrous, anarchic, and violent; they were without any civil and religious laws. The Holy Koran, as revealed to them by their Prophet, is a statement on the supremacy of ethical life and the dignity of man. This Holy Book reveals the same truths that are dear to Christians in the Gospels and to Jews in the Torah: filial duty, chastity, the inviolable sanctity of human life and property, social integrity, and the purity of sentiment.[1] The central theme of Islam is the oneness of God, and on this score Muslims are similar to Jews. Christianity is seen by Muslims as a polytheistic religion because of the Christian doctrine of the Trinity. Islam repudiates Jesus Christ as an all-human, all-divine savior-- merely treating Christ as one of many prophets.

Fundamentally, all Mideastern societies were merchant societies, dreading unruly chaos and anarchy, and striving to maintain an authoritarian order with strong leadership. The population was frightened when control from above was eliminated, and the tribes and sects ended up fighting with one another. This also occurred in medieval Europe. Obedience to the despot, no matter how illegitimate that despot may have been, was often preferable, particularly in Arab society, to anarchy. There is an ancient Arabic expression that says: "Better 60 years of tyranny than one day of anarchy." The Christian reader will find passages in the New Testament where Christ implores his disciples to distinguish between the religious and the secular: sovereigns, kings, and civil authorities. "What belongs to Caesar is Caesar's, and what is God's is God's."

Tribalism and authoritarianism not only characterize the politics of Saddam Hussein in Iraq, but of Hafez al-Assad in Syria. Al-Assad belongs to the Alawite sect, a tributary of Shi'ism ruling over a predominantly Sunni Arab majority in Syria. This explains his easy alliance with the Shi'ites in Iran. It will also explain how the ruler of Syria, Hafez al-Assad, could have 20,000 of his own citizens killed in the town of Hama. These Syrians were sacrificed not because they were Sunni Arabs, but because al-Assad considered them Muslim fanatics and members of an alien tribe.

Saddam Hussein, on the other hand, belongs to the Takrit sect (or tribe). Takrit is a village situated north of Baghdad on the Tigris River. The real name of Iraqi president Saddam Hussein is therefore Saddam Hussein al-Takriti. All the chief conspirators who came to power in the wings of the Ba'ath party in the 1968 coup came from the village of Takrit. Any relative of theirs who lived anywhere near Takrit simply appended "al-Takriti" to his name; the Iraqi regime thus became affiliated with the Takriti sect. There is a preponderance of Takritis in the army and the intelligence agencies, and the key posts in the Ba'ath party are all occupied by Takritis.

The great Kurdish general Saladin was also born and reared in Takrit. Iraqi Arabs have consistently played up this point, although Saddam and the Iraqi regime never refer to Saladin's Kurdish origins. In the mid-1970s, Saddam ordered the state-controlled media not to call his followers "al-Takriti" anymore. The president's name henceforth became simply Saddam Hussein. Whatever the reason behind the name change, for it ceased to really matter all that much to himself or his men, Israel Radio's Arabic Service (*Kol Yisrael*) facetiously continued to call the Iraqi leader "Saddam Hussein al-Takriti," to poke fun at him and to remind the Iraqi people of the tribal character of the Iraqi regime.

HOW SADDAM HUSSEIN ACHIEVED UNITY FOR IRAQ

One of the results of the pervasiveness of Islam is the importance that has long been attached to unity in the Mideastern political scene. The Arab people have historically been unified by their common land, economy, language, race, culture, religion, and history, even if they were divided along sectarian lines.

The concept of Arab unity can be traced to the 1940s and the Syrian Ba'ath party's call for Arab unification from the Atlantic Ocean to the Persian Gulf. Libyan leader Muammar Qaddafi once stated that his dream of Arab unity is "a hope shared by all Arab people. Even Arab rulers, although in principle opposed to it because it threatens their personal power, still pay lip-service to these popular aspirations."[2] At bottom, Qaddafi is no less a pan-Arabist than Saddam. Qaddafi, too, believes that all Arab nations should be a single Arab state. He has always felt that regionalism is a political result of colonialism, which served to allow the West to control the Middle East.

The Ba'ath party also forms the governing party in Iraq. It was created in 1953 from the merger of two vanguard parties: the Arab Resurrectionist party (founded in 1947 by Michel Aflaq and Salah al-Din Bitar) and the Socialist party (founded in 1950 by Akram Hourani). The Ba'ath was essentially created as "a national, populist, revolutionary movement fighting for Arab unity, freedom, and socialism;"[3] it was meant to reawaken Arab nationalism and to rebuild socialism in an Arab form. Only those ignorant of history and lacking political discernment will say this is normal and the best thing that could ever happen to a people who had seen the fetters of colonialism.

But the Iraqis deserve much better than what they got. What they actually got more or less amounts to an Arab form of national socialism, or nazism. No self-respecting Arab nationalist, no matter how conscious he is of past oppression and foreign tyranny, could possibly agree that what Saddam has offered could be anything remotely resembling socialism. That being said, how could a perverted nationalism, tinged with Arab tribalism, be considered "nationalism" in the true sense of the word? The only qualification I can offer in justification of Saddam's political regime is that *nationalism* is such an abstract term that it follows criteria that cannot be set down by Westerners alone. The nationalism of any nation is linked to the ill-begotten myths that that nation allows itself to be ruled by. In scope and in vision, this is a purely subjective notion.

At first glance, the constitution of the Arab Resurrection Socialist party is a democratic document attesting to many of the ideals held dear in the West and in high esteem by all Arab nationalists as well. One of these ideals is the unification of the Arabs and speaks of fundamental freedoms of speech, belief, and assembly. They also seek to throw off the yoke of Western colonialism and assert themselves as a unified, homogeneous people who are responsible for their own welfare.[4]

Yet all the power of the Iraqi people lies entirely in the hands of Saddam Hussein and his inner circle, called the Revolutionary Command Council. Thus the Ba'ath party and the Command Council are really indistinguishable from Hussein himself. With few exceptions, only members of his family or people from his village have been placed in high positions. Saddam has virtually wiped out any independent thought that might in some way oppose him within the Ba'ath party. Saddam Hussein became little more than a dictator, a man who needed an organization to work with, an army to build, a foreign policy to follow, and a supporting cast to follow him.

There is an interesting analogy with Hitler's crackdown in the *Nationalsozialistische Deutsche Arbeiterpartei* or NSDAP (National Socialist German Workers' Party) during the famous "Night of the Long Knives." Hitler had used the S.S. (*Schutzstauffel*) to rid himself of his potential rivals in the Nazi S.A. (*Sturmabteilung*) before it was too late and before the S.A. could secure control of the German army. By mid-1979, Saddam had been the number-two man in Ba'ath politics for a period of 11 years. President Ahmed Hasan al-Bakr was ailing. For a number of years Saddam had been groomed to become the president of Iraq. Unfortunately, for him, or so he thought, there were about five people in the Ba'ath party who could have blocked his ascension to the top post in the party and government.

So, with an uncommon brutality, on July 16, 1979, Saddam had one of these opponents--a certain Muhyi Abd al-Husain al-Mashhadi, the Ba'ath party's secretary-general, obviously not of the Takriti clan, arrested. He was mercilessly tortured until a false confession had been wrung out of him and he admitted to plotting the ouster of Saddam from the party with the help of some others. But who were the other ringleaders? It was said that Syria was involved in the affair. Rumor had it that there were a number of Iraqi Ba'athists who were anxious to consummate the union with the Syrian Ba'athists.

A week later, Saddam convened an extraordinary ad-hoc meeting of the Iraqi Ba'ath party Regional Congress to hear al-Mashhadi's confession in full view of the whole assembly. It was a grotesque stage performance; the whole scene was filmed. It reminded one of the tactics of the Israeli Mossad (secret police) which went about its operation filming the execution of a Palestinian leader so that Israeli intelligence agents, viewing the whole picture on video cassettes, could later see and learn how it was all done.

In a graphic example of intimidation, Saddam sat up at the front of the hall, taking big puffs on his cigar. He had stage-managed the episode to suit an obedient audience. As al-Mashhadi went through the process of mentioning the names of the others in the plot, each person was forced to stand up. A guard would then come along and drag him from the assembly hall. The co-conspirators referred to were: Mohammed Ayish, Mohammed Mahjub, Husayn al-Hamdani, and Ghanim Abd al-Jalil--all members of Iraq's ruling Revolutionary Command Council. All the conspirators stood at attention, their knees shaking, their faces sullen, as the guards spirited them away one by one. Al-Hamdani was heartbroken and wept. He had been one of Saddam's closest friends and felt betrayed.

After that riveting spectacle, seventeen other bogus conspirators were found guilty and sentenced to death. The executions were done with sub-machine guns--Saddam conspicuously participating, taking the liberty of nonchalantly firing the first volley. In one month, videotapes of this grisly event were distributed to all regional Ba'ath party branches, and to most army units; a few copies eventually ended up in Kuwait and Beirut. The BBC got hold of one and aired it on prime-time only after Saddam's seizure of Kuwait in 1990. No one, strangely enough, thought of exposing the sadism of Saddam's "democracy" any sooner.

IRAQ AND THE WEST

The last important characteristic of Iraq and the pan-Arab designs of Saddam Hussein was the influence of Western imperialism in Iraq, particularly during the British colonial period.

The great writers on Arab culture and history seem to agree on the Arabs' general hatred of the West and of Western ways. The great Islamist historian Bernard Lewis once called it a "cultural inferiority complex," even among modernizing Arabs. The Israeli Arabist Raphael Patai was no less perplexed when he compared the Arabs with the Indians of the subcontinent. "The peoples [of the subcontinent]...," he mused, "were under British rule for two centuries. Their relationship to Britain during that period," he found, "was similar to the relationship of the Arab states to Britain or to France from the end of World War I." "Nevertheless," Patai concludes, "in India and in Muslim Pakistan one finds little of the hatred of Britain or of the West that characterizes the Arab states."[5] If we believe that most Arabs suffer in fact from a latent "inferiority complex," then Western influences were historically very profound and Western culture has been overwhelmingly intrusive and dominant. To the extent there is any inferiority complex, assuming we accept this at face value, this cannot be chalked off solely to the colonial and post-colonial experiences of the Arabs. Indeed, it lies in the incongruity of their past experiences--greatness followed by decline.

For most articulate Arabs, the distant past offers inspiring memories of splendor and glory. Twelve hundred years ago the Arab Empire was the greatest in the world, stretching from the Indus Valley (of India) to the Atlantic. The past was marked by conquest, aggressiveness, scholarship, and bravery, ideals that to many Arabs have been absent for too long. The realities of today are different. These ideals are to be rebuilt and remade in a new consciousness. There is thus an inclination to emulate the ancestral ways. Present-day Egyptians often invoke the pharaohs of antiquity. Tunisians hark back to Carthage before it was razed to the ground by Roman legions. Modern Iraqis would like to relive a new Babylon.

When the West flaunts its superior technical and military power, the Arabs tend to feel culturally inferior. It seems dishonoring and degrading to have the Western upstarts dictate a new scale of values. Israel is often seen as having adapted itself more successfully than any Arab country to the ways of the West. Thus Israel exists, in the Arab mind, as a denial of the Arab past, present, and future. In six major wars against the Hebrew state, the Arabs suffered defeat in each one. Hence the hatred of the West and the enmity toward Israel.

These features soon became part and parcel of the mythology of the Iraqi Ba'ath party, of the Iraqi regime, and were perpetuated by President Saddam Hussein. Iraq has gone through a long and venerable history of great civilizations, impacting not only on the region but the world. The Sumerians, who ruled in the third millennium B.C., developed writing, urban culture, and an administrative bureaucracy. After the Sumerians, two civilizations were to rise and rule over this land during the second millennium B.C. First came Babylon, unrivaled in the splendor of the ancient world. The Babylonians were noted for many cultural and scientific achievements. Here were the Hanging Gardens of Semiramis, one of the seven wonders of the civilized world. Nebuchadnezzar fought successful wars. One of the other Babylonian kings, Hammurabi, codified what was essentially one of the first known principles of social jurisprudence--legal documents that are still in use. Next came the fierce and rapacious Assyrians, who developed the concept of a standing army that was controlled by a permanent political bureaucracy. These two empires eventually collapsed around 500 B.C. In the subsequent centuries, Iraq succumbed to the rule of various Greek and Persian dynasties until the final conquest of Mesopotamia in the seventh century by an Arab-Muslim army on the battlefield of al-Qadissiya. A new era had dawned on Iraq. Persian power was on the wane, and Islam was beginning to make significant inroads on Middle Eastern history.

The Abbasids (who ruled from A.D. 750 to 1258) ruled an empire stretching from their capital at Baghdad to Afghanistan in the east and as far as North Africa in the west. They encouraged the admixture of Persian, Greek, and Arab cultures and languages. They stressed the sciences of mathematics, chemistry, astronomy, and medicine and made lasting contributions to cartography and literature, translating the ancient works of the Greeks and Romans into Arabic. In 1258 this empire was conquered by the Mongols, and in the sixteenth century the Ottoman Turks took over.

Iraq was thus at a crossroads between the Turks and the Persians and, in the end, became an outlying region of the Ottoman Empire, benefiting precious little from Ottoman rule, except in the way of clearly marked administrative regions divided along ethnic/linguistic/racial lines without any geographic frontiers. These divisions were called "*vilayets.*" Kurds, Sunni Arabs, Shi'a Arabs, Christian Assyrians, Armenians, Nestorians, and so forth, were demarcated according to these "*vilayets.*" It was a very practical form of geographic separation, for the Ottomans had absolutely no conception of a Mideastern possession or territory.

The very concept of the "Middle East" had been foreign to the Arabs, too. The word in effect exists in Arabic: *Al-sharq al-awsat*, but the notion was first adapted from the original French and English concepts of "*Proche-Orient*" and "Mideast." The state of modern Iraq was effectively first conceived by the secret Sykes-Picot agreement of 1916, which divided the Ottoman Empire between the British and the French. When the Ottoman Empire finally crumbled, the British merged three former Ottoman provinces to form Iraq. How did the British do it? And why did they do it?

The answers are straightforward. The British literally took out a blank sheet of paper and traced a map of the area, as if they were drawing lines in the sand, which was what it really amounted to. Sir Percy Cox, the British High Commissioner, drew the boundaries separating Saudi Arabia from Kuwait and Kuwait from Iraq. The borders were thus all artificial, creating, as it were, nation-states out of a region where previously there had been none. The "lines in the sand" were all polygons, drawn at right angles with little regard for ethnic, tribal, linguistic, or religious realities that had been reflected in the Ottoman *"vilayet"* delimitations. Out of the blue, these nation-states were saddled with the trappings and the organizations of a British liberal democracy--parliaments, constitutions, national anthems, cabinets, and political parties. Iraq, for instance, south of the Shatt-al-Arab River estuary, was given only a 36-kilometer shoreline, hardly enough to build a second port. Besides, the boundaries were made on the basis of British foreign policy, with a view to dominating the region's communications and its oil-bearing regions. Britain had already acquired an economic concession in Iran called the Anglo-Persian Oil Company, where she alone was left in charge of the exploitation, the refinement, and the marketing of that new and important commodity--oil.

If the artificiality of the borders were not enough, the British imposed the rulers they thought fit on these newly created oil states of the Persian Gulf. In Saudi Arabia it was the Saud tribe, in Kuwait the al-Sabah family, in Jordan the Hashemites, in Iraq the Hashemite cousins as well. The British, moreover, gave names to these states, including the name Palestine, which to the local Arabs had no precedent in their history as referring to a distinct Palestinian territory. The French did the same thing; in Lebanon they set up the Christian Maronites as the dominant group. It was only a question of time before there were wide-scale rebellions and ethnic, tribal, and village authorities began to assert themselves. Britain (and France), after all, could not control, let alone keep, this region forever.

What with tribal, sectarian, and regional loyalties stronger than any artificial sense of statehood, in Iraq three different communities were literally thrown together. The Kurds live in the north; they are a large ethnic community whose population straddles a southern tip of the former Soviet Union and covers parts of Turkey, Syria, Iran, and Iraq. The Kurds have always longed for their own independent state, and they were promised one at the end of World War I by the Treaty of Sèvres the Kurds are markedly different from the Arab Iraqis. Their origins are patently Indo-European, closer to the Iranians than to the Semitic races. Like the majority of Arabs, however, the Kurds are Sunni Muslims. Their struggle in Iraq is precisely against the Sunni Arabs who rule Iraq under the strong hand of Saddam Hussein. But there is a semantic variation on the theme of Kurdish independence. As Mas'ud Barzani, the present leader of the Kurdish Democratic party, stated in 1985: "We will live with the Arab people [in the state of Iraq], but not with a dictatorial regime."[6] Besides, the Kurds of Iraq sit atop an extraordinarily petroliferous area near Mosul and Kirkuk. The British did not want the Turks to acquire this region (once a part of the Ottoman Empire), so they incorporated it into the nascent Iraqi state.

Real power in Iraq belongs, has indeed always belonged, to the Sunni minority, and this power has always been autocratic. The Sunni minority's control of the state of Iraq was typical of the governments formed in each of the states created by the British and French. For example, as the Sunnis dominate Iraq, the Alawites have tended to dominate Syria, the Saud tribe dominates Saudi Arabia, and the British-appointed kingship of the Hashemites rules over the Kingdom of Jordan, whose population is Bedouin and Palestinian.

The British authorities installed the Hashemite King Faisal as the first Iraqi king in what was supposed to be a constitutional monarchy. Faisal and his advisors were above all Sunni. One Mideast expert, Thomas Friedman, has written:

> Aside from a genuine commitment to principles of self-determination and dignity for their country, their support for Arab nationalism linked Iraq to the broader, Sunni-dominated, Arab world and served as a rationale for perpetuating their rule over a country whose majority was not Sunni Arab.[7]

Hence the newborn Iraqi nation was split along ethnic and religious lines. As a result, the Kurds and Shi'ites of Iraq periodically rebel against the regime in Baghdad.

In 1932, Iraq became the first Arab state, after Saudi Arabia, to gain its independence. It became the first Arab state to join the League of Nations. Meanwhile Britain reserved the right, in her old colonial fashion, to maintain military bases on Iraq's soil. The move was intended to safeguard British oil interests. In 1933 Faisal died. His successor, Ghazi, turned out to be an extremely weak leader, passing from the scene in 1939, at around the time World War II broke out. And the Germans, not surprisingly, had now decided to reenter the political game in the Middle East. The Germans were no strangers to this area. Under the Kaiser Wilhelm, they had planned the construction of the Berlin-Baghdad railway. Railroads were the best method of penetrating the Middle East, and the Hohenzollern Empire availed itself of this opportunity with the consent of their Ottoman allies. From Baghdad, that railway was to be extended to Basra and from there on to Kuwait. Coming to power in Germany in 1933, Hitler resurrected this old German "*drang nach Süden.*" Oil played an important part too. The Germans needed oil so badly because without it they could not successfully prosecute and win their "lightning war". The only obstacle to Germany's path in the Middle East was British control of the oil resources. The Nazis consequently did not waste any time courting the Iraqis, since they thought Iraq was ideally suited to unite the Arabs behind Nazi Germany. For their part, the Iraqis saw Arab, Sunni-dominated fascism as a form of revenge for having been done in by the British.

During World War II, Iraq was suddenly split into three ideological parts: the Communists tended to be the Kurds and the Shi'ites, including other minorities; the Arab nationalists were primarily middle and upper-class Sunnis; and the members of the Ba'ath party, then surreptitiously waiting in the wings, held sway over the lower-class Sunnis and some Shi'ites. An Iraqi officer named Rashid Ali, aided and abetted by German agents and prompted by the Shah of Iran, who was also pro-Nazi, masterminded a coup in Habbaniyah in 1940. Following its suppression, all Iraqi officers were summarily dismissed. Iraq, like Iran, was occupied by the British, and ultimately, albeit reluctantly, Baghdad declared war on Germany in 1943.

During the East-West Cold War years, Soviet expansion southward was considered to be the main threat to the region's security. The West could not permit any of these Arab, or Muslim, states to fall to the lure of Communism. The Americans and the British consequently conceived of an additional link to the much-vaunted North Atlantic Treaty Organization (NATO) system. It was called the Baghdad Pact and was set up in 1955. One could say that Iraq was almost forced to join this pact, which was little more than a military alliance binding Iraq closer to Britain, Turkey, Iran, and Pakistan. Iraq easily became a member of this pro-Western alliance; in fact, Iraq was the linchpin in the treaty. It could not be otherwise, since the Hashemite king was still in power and the king owed his power to the British. But that was all going to change, and very soon.

In 1958, General Abdul Karim Qassim staged a military coup and overthrew the monarchy. An Arab nationalist, Qassim's ancestry in Iraq was unique. His father was a Sunni Arab; his mother was a Shi'a Kurd. Oddly enough, he concluded an alliance with the Iraqi Communists, who helped him overthrow the pro-British Hashemites. But Qassim quickly turned against his erstwhile allies, realizing that the Communists would keep their allegiance to Moscow. Not everyone seemed to like Qassim, and for many reasons. There were several attempts on Qassim's life: sometimes he was singled out by the Kurds, at other times by the Iraqi Communists, most frequently, though, by members of the rapidly rising Ba'ath party. Qassim was a marked man the moment he came to power; when it would all end for him was just a matter of time.[8]

The tocsin finally sounded on February 8, 1963, when Qassim was overthrown and Colonel Abdul-Salam Arif (the leader of the nationalists) became president. Al-Bakr, the Ba'athist, became prime minister. But the Ba'athists alone took credit for Qassim's assassination. It was rumored that the American CIA orchestrated the coup, banking on the Ba'athists, in view of Washington's fear of Iraqi Communist subversion. A few years before, the CIA had put the Iranian Shah back on his throne, fearing the Iranian Communists. The population found it unbelievable that a popular hero like Qassim could be liquidated without much ado. Masters of conspiracy and propaganda, the Ba'athists responded to the public outcry by transmitting pictures of his bullet-riddled body on television. Qassim was shown sitting down at a desk in his private studio. An Iraqi soldier walked up to the half-mutilated corpse, seized the dead man's hair, while pointing to the mouth as it lolled wide open, and spat right into it. It was a macabre spectacle, typical of the bestiality of Mideast politics.

That was not the end of it. In 1966, Arif died in a mysterious helicopter accident and was succeeded by his brother, Abdul Rahman Arif. On July 17, 1968, the Ba'ath party seized power again, and this time it appeared it was for good. This time they were directly assisted by the Iraqi army and army intelligence. The deputy director of military intelligence, Colonel Abd al-Razzaq al-Nayif, became prime minister. The commander of the elite Iraqi Republican Guard was Colonel Ibrahim al-Daud; he became defense minister. Their tenure was short-lived, however. Real power lay with al-Bakr and the slippery gray eminence now waiting in the wings of the regime--Saddam Hussein.

NOTES

1. The Koran, like the Bible containing the Old and New Testaments, may not have originated in Mohammed's lifetime. In my book *Iran at the Crossroads: Global Relations in a Turbulent Decade* (Boulder: Westview, 1990), I have indicated that modern scholars, using methods adapted from Biblical analysis, suggest that the Koran, as we know it, might well have been assembled some time after the Arab conquest of the Middle East, from a large body of oral literature as a result of continuing polemics with Christians and Jews (pp. 203-204).

2. Mahmoud M. Ayoub, *Islam and the Third Universal Theory: The Religious Thought of Mu'ammar al-Qadhdhafi* (London: KPI, 1987), p. 24.

3. Manfred Halpern, *The Politics of Social Change in the Middle East and North Africa* (Princeton, N.J.: Princeton University Press, 1963), p. 240.

4. "The Constitution of the Arab Resurrection Socialist Party," in Sami A. Hanna and George H. Gardner, eds., *Arab Socialism--A Documentary Survey* (Leiden, Netherlands: E. J. Brill, 1969), p. 306.

5. Raphael Patai, *The Arab Mind*, revised ed. (New York: Charles Scribner's and Sons, 1983), pp. 296-297.

6. See Shahram Chubin and Charles Tripp, *Iran and Iraq at War* (Boulder: Westview, 1988), p. 104.

7. Thomas Friedman, *From Beirut to Jerusalem* (New York: Anchor Books, 1989), p. 69.

8. For a recent, well-balanced account of Qassim, see Robert A. Fernes and William Roger Louis, eds., *The Iraqi Revolution of 1958* (London: I. B. Taurus and St. Martin's Press, 1991).

2

"Standing Steadfast"

Who can this Saddam Hussein be? Where did he come from? Is this the Sadim of Babel, once prophesied in medieval Arabic's love and lore? Why has he been characterized as an heir to Saladin, the next Nebuchadnezzar, a Stalin, a Mideast Hitler, loved and loathed at the same time?

His name in Arabic means "standing steadfast." Saddam Hussein al-Takriti was born to Hussein al-Majid and his wife, Subha, on April 28, 1937. Conflicting stories continue to surface about Saddam's father. Iraqi sources say that he died soon after Saddam was born. Others contend that the father left Subha soon after Saddam came into the world or that he never married Subha at all. Whichever story is true, Saddam grew up in a frightful environment, abused and browbeaten by his stepfather, Ibrahim al-Hassan al-Takriti, his father's brother. Other accounts say that Saddam was unbearably teased by the other village children with respect to his supposed illegitimacy and took out his frustrations with an iron bar or a pistol. This, in itself, may explain a great deal about the shaping of his character. While still young, he was determined to finish school and ran away from home to live with his uncle Khairallah Tulfah.

As he grew older, Saddam became more and more involved in politics. While still in school, he is said to have murdered a man involved in an inter-clan dispute. Saddam also murdered the leader of the local Communist party, who happened to be his own brother-in-law. In 1956 he apparently took part in one of the unsuccessful revolts against the king of Iraq. A year later he joined the Ba'ath party as an activist. He won a reputation as a campus bully, a heckler and troublemaker at meetings organized by the nationalists, Communists, or any of the other groups that were slowly emerging in the new political climate.

Over the years, Saddam proved to be less and less noisy, and growing out of his formative years he became more and more taciturn. He seemed almost invented for Arab leadership. He appeared more modern in outlook than the other Ba'athists--cool, correct, handsome, and, by Arab standards, a man of considerable stature. Although never mastering any foreign language, he cut an imposing figure among his peers. Developing a taste for luxury items is not perhaps in itself a strange habit for successful Arab politicians and statesmen, but Saddam's penchant was not for automobiles or gold; he liked the trendy fashions of Europe. When faced with undue stress or hardship, he would not flinch, never directly showing the slightest emotion, keeping his upper and lower lips stiff in defiance. His name seemed to fit well with his personality.

When the Hashemite monarchy was overthrown, Saddam joined a group that tried to murder the new leader of Iraq, General Abdul Karim Qassim. When the assassination attempt failed, legend has it, Hussein sustained a serious wound and fled to Syria, eventually ending up in Egypt, where he finished high school and married his uncle Khairallah's daughter--Sajida. Other sources say he was only slightly wounded by one of his own comrades and abandoned the others to be captured while he fled.

When Qassim was toppled, Saddam returned to Iraq and became an interrogator (and torturer) under the Ba'ath government. Between 1964 and 1966, Saddam spent some time in prison. When released, he rose through the Ba'ath hierarchy and was appointed to the Ba'ath regional command by Michel Aflaq, the "spiritual" leader of the Ba'ath party, himself. Saddam then proceeded to build up the *Jihaz Haneen* ("instrument of yearning"), which became the party's internal security apparatus, later renamed the *Mukhabarat*, or the General Intelligence Department. Eventually, Saddam's half-brother Sabaawi Ibrahim headed the *Mukhabarat* and it was divided into a number of sections, including Military Intelligence (*'Alistikhbarat al-A'askariyah*), and foreign espionage operations (*Jihaz al-Amn al-Kharji*). In 1965, Saddam's cousin, General Ahmad Hassan al-Bakr, became secretary-general of the Ba'ath party, and it was he who appointed Saddam deputy secretary-general in 1966. Saddam's wife, who was to bear him five children, helped him seal the relationship between him and al-Bakr by inducing al-Bakr's son to marry her sister and two of his daughters to marry two of her brothers. Whatever power they were after, they were obviously going to keep it in an extended family.

In 1968 the Ba'ath party seized power in Iraq. Ahmad Hassan al-Bakr became president and Saddam was made deputy chairman of the Revolutionary Command Council in 1970. Under al-Bakr's government, Saddam used his position to concentrate on his own personal power and rid himself of all real, potential, imagined, or contrived political rivals. In October of 1968, for example, the Ba'ath government announced that it had smashed a Zionist spy ring. After a perfunctory show trial, the 17 "spies" were sentenced and 14 of them were hung. This was tantamount to waving a red rag at an angry Zionist state.

American authors Judith Miller and Laurie Mylroie, who came out with the first interesting book on Saddam after his invasion of Kuwait, point out that the "Jews had been a stepping-stone to the regime's real target."[1] Saddam wasted no time in executing Muslims as well, including influential members of the party hierarchy, who suddenly found themselves powerless. Real power came to be centered in Hussein's hands when al-Bakr resigned in 1979, citing health reasons and clearing the way for Saddam to go all the way to the top. Many in Iraq who were opposed to Saddam for personal reasons were quick to point out that al-Bakr was forced into retirement by a politically dominant Hussein and may even have been murdered by Hussein's henchmen.

Thus in July 1979, Saddam became president of Iraq and chairman of the Revolutionary Command Council. Simultaneously, he also became the chairman of the Council of Ministers, the commander in chief of the armed forces, general secretary of the Regional Command of the Arab Ba'ath Socialist Party (ABSP), chairman of the Supreme Planning Council, chairman of the Committee on Agreements, chairman of the Supreme Agricultural Council, and chairman of the Supreme Council for the Compulsory Eradication of Illiteracy.[2] In 1977, the absorption of the Ba'ath Regional Command into the Revolutionary Command Council ended the existence of the Ba'ath party as an independent body--a step that Hussein claimed was designed to deepen collective participation and democracy. Analysts agree, however, that this step was more in the line of co-opting those who might one day pose a threat to Hussein's power.[3]

Saddam Hussein is not one who is able to trust anyone but his closest relatives and tribal members whom he would not regard as a direct threat. On one occasion, however, even a family member was suspected of disloyalty and killed. Adnan Khairallah, his bosom friend and cousin, lost his life in a freak helicopter accident, or at least what appeared to be an accident, not long after he criticized Saddam's treatment of the Kurds in the north. Realizing Adnan was popular in the regime, Saddam ordered a state funeral for him, and it was rumored that Iraq's new president was crestfallen for many weeks. Since then he has tried to maintain a close inner circle of confidants.

Two British writers, in one of the earlier books on Saddam Hussein, have observed that there is a simple logic behind this: "All Iraqis are one family, the godfather is Saddam Hussein, therefore any form of dissent is an act of treason; traitors must be punished."[4] Ideas of clannishness are close to Saddam's heart; it is said of him that the American film *The Godfather*, with Marlon Brando, is as much a favorite of his as *The Great Gatsby*, with Robert Redford, was for the executed rulers of Romania, Nicolae Ceausescu and his wife, Yelena.

Saddam believes that he always speaks for the Iraqi people. Their wishes are his. When he purged the Revolutionary Command Council, the Ba'ath party, and the Ministries during the Ninth Ba'ath Party Regional Congress in 1982, Saddam was able to establish some consistency of views in the party. It was a consistency with his own views, of course, based on the assumption (or presumption) that he was the head of the Iraqi state and ipso facto his wishes were the wishes of the people. All power in Iraq had effectively become associated with this single individual. He was to be equated with the state, analogous to King Louis XIV of France, who once said, "*L'état c'est moi*" ("I am the state").

CHIMERAS, IDEALS, AND REALITIES

Arab society has traditionally been male-oriented; it is both patrilineal and patriarchal. While women are better off in Iraq than in the Arab monarchies, they are still treated as second-class citizens, guarded, if not altogether sequestered, lest they bring dishonor to their fathers, husbands, or brothers through sexual misconduct. Men are cherished from the moment they are born. To learn courage, sons are often taught to be strong by being whipped and beaten. But in all this, the ideal family, like the ideal society in the Arab mind, is an extended one.

These ideals may be extended to Saddam himself. Saddam grew up without a support structure under a brutal stepfather; he was later dependent on his uncle. It is very possible that because he grew up without one he sees the nation as an extended family: a family that needs to be firmly brought together in order to survive. He must obviously see himself as a "patriarch," the wisest of all, the grandfather who must lead his people, the leader who must settle disputes. The Republican Guards could be interpreted as representing his favored sons who are loyal only to Hussein, their father. And what can a father do to keep a feuding family together? Saddam clings to the view that the Shi'ites and the Kurds, like Arab women guilty of having committed sexual indiscretions, are likely to bring dishonor to the country. When indiscretions are committed, familial justice must be meted out. The connection between Arab ideals and Saddam's ideals raises a number of fascinating questions.

Having assumed total power, Saddam began to cultivate the idea that the will of the people was the most important political ideal of all. If Saddam represented the state of Iraq and if one day Saddam were to fall, so too would Iraq. It was generally felt that defending Saddam meant defending Iraq. War was justifiable on these grounds. All those who spoke out against him were opposing the will of the people and committing treason. He skillfully defined national pride using the old Arabic term *shu'ubbiya*. It is one of those genuinely untranslatable words, compacted with several layers of meaning. Samir al-Khalil says that *Shu'ubism* is a thought process that allows all Arabs, and Arab nationalists in particular, to define who the Arabs' enemy really is. He writes: "Just as history's *Shu'ubi* was not only a Persian, today's *Shu'ubis* in Iraq can be communists, minorities and Shi'ites."[5]

Saddam Hussein has often been called a thug and a man without leadership qualities. He is neither. Saddam had no army experience; his grades in school were not sufficiently high enough to admit him to the Baghdad Military Academy. Without this army experience, he has shown an exemplary discipline. With nerves of steel, literally behind the backs of the Iraqi General Staff, he had himself appointed lieutenant-general in 1976, then field-marshal the moment war broke out with Iran. He used this position to aggregate to himself many military and academic honors, including an honorary degree in law. During the war that pitted him against the Allies in 1991, General Schwarzkopf, the commander of the Allied effort, described him in these terms: "He is neither a strategist, nor is he schooled in the operational art, nor is he a tactician, nor is he a general, nor is he a soldier. Other than that, he's a great military man."[6]

The epithets ascribed to the Iraqi dictator are revealing, for they point to a man of extraordinary insight and *sang froid*. Saddam Hussein may not have read or found time to read George Antonius's 1938 classic, *The Arab Awakening*, to understand the yearning of the Arab spirit. Yet his sense of Arab nationalism was always very acute. He has often referred to the ancient battle of al-Qaddissiya, when the Arabs first defeated the Persians. Consider the simplicity and power of Saddam's style of speech: "The glory of the Arabs stems from the glory of Iraq. Throughout history, whenever Iraq became mighty and flourished, so did the Arab nation."[7]

Saddam was neither a fool nor could he suffer fools. There is a strong element of calculation in his actions that points to considerable intellectual powers. He will tolerate no wild irrationality, deviousness, maliciousness, and venality in others. He will not allow others to criticize his assumptions, and he is known to be mean and cruel when disrupted or disagreed with.

When stress was too great for him at the height of the Iran-Iraq war, it was said that he had one of his doctors killed, and had the body cut into tiny pieces and then delivered to the doctor's family because the doctor suggested that Saddam should rest and delegate some of the authority. Saddam's distrust is too easily aroused. Vindictive, coarse, and sadistic, he is known to take pleasure in the misfortunes of his enemies. He has always believed in a mission of the Arab nation, in that it was destined to fulfil a messianic role in world history. Saddam could never allow himself to be self-deprecating and often beguiles a visitor with a profound exterior calm, then ending on an optimistic note indicating that all will be alright, that the future is promising.

Whatever words Saddam uses, whatever pronouncements his government makes, they are typical of a proclivity among most Arabs for verbal exaggeration. The Arabs on the whole have had a long-standing infatuation with ideal forms and exaggerated concepts, with things occult and supernatural, even though they know such phenomena to be contradicted by hard-nosed reality.

The Arab style of speech has had something to do with this. Word forms in Arabic easily lend themselves to overstatement. One need only listen to most Arab leaders' speeches. Metaphoric phrases like *mother of all battles* are purely rhetorical, and they are often misinterpreted and misunderstood by people in the West. Such language may be interpreted by the uninitiated as arrogant overconfidence, as false bravado; in fact, it is merely a characteristic of Arab literary speech.

In addition to acquiring a vocabulary and grammar, every Arab child acquires specific stylistic devices of speech that are not readily present in Western cultures. One is known as "*mubalagha*" (exaggeration); the other is "*tawkid*" (over-assertion). Arab speech patterns place greater emphasis on appearance than on meaning. Saddam Hussein is hardly an exception when he speaks Arabic. In effect, his Arabic shows a predilection for repetition and a tendency to announce actions or events as if they were already an accomplished fact. Palestinian leader Yasser Arafat speaks in the same way; at times what he says in Arabic is semantically different from what he says in English. Western interlocutors often stand aghast at this manner of conducting public relations. When one reads into Saddam Hussein's embellished exaggerations, one will notice that his statements are seldom followed by serious or sustained efforts to translate them into action. When he does translate words into action, he prepares the subversive groundwork very cautiously, leaving nothing to chance, making doubly sure he has covered his rear. His only mistakes are his miscalculations. The reader will discover this further on in the narrative when we assess Saddam's actions at the height of the two Gulf wars.

A mystique shrouds the personality of Saddam Hussein. He is said to take special delight in exaggerating his own apotheosis, even making his birthday a national holiday. He has rewritten his family tree to show his descent from the Prophet. This has an enormous impact on Muslims and Arabs everywhere. Qaddafi believes he is descended from the same Prophet; so at one time did the Ayatollah Khomeini. And King Hussein of Jordan still says and believes the holy cities draw their legitimacy from the Prophet of Islam. Mecca and Medina were not long ago fiefs of the deposed Hashemite clan in the Hejaz. King Hussein of Jordan belongs to that Hashemite clan.

In order to further his own myth, Saddam has been involved in various books and movies excerpted from events occurring in his own life. There have been at least two very laudatory books written about him: Amir Iskandar's *Saddam Hussein: The Fighter, the Thinker and the Man* and Fouad Matar's *Saddam Hussein: A Biography*. He has also been involved in a film called *Aliyam Altawilah* (The Long Days): a film that "was a dramatisation, using top box-office stars, of the life and super-heroic deeds of Saddam Hussein, his struggle to build the Ba'ath party and to create a modern Iraq."[8]

Yet his power and prestige have not made Saddam any less insecure or less paranoid. He takes a food taster wherever he goes, and all his visitors are searched before they are let in to see him. In order to assure the complete loyalty of his bodyguards, Saddam married his daughter Raghd to the commander of his bodyguards, Hussein Kamel. Saddam's whim for out-of-bounds exaggeration brooked no bounds. A graphic example is the way his roving eye glimpsed the graceful Samira Shahbandar, the wife of Nurredin al-Safi. Whether or not she was in love with her husband did not matter to Saddam, for the Iraqi leader asked al-Safi to let him have his wife. Saddam was overjoyed and delighted he could take another wife, and why not? Muslim law would allow him as many as four. Saddam rewarded al-Safi's unusual gesture by giving him the directorship of the company he had been representing--*Iraqi Airways*.

This ruthless ruler of Iraq has for more than a decade been perceived as a hero by most Arabs. Saladin and Nebuchadnezzar and Hammurabi could not have restored the magic and majesty of the city of Babylon any better. On February 8, 1979, Saddam issued the "Pan-Arab Charter" (later dubbed the "Hussein Doctrine"), which called for a collective Arab defense and the rejection of any Western presence in the Gulf and resulted in Arab support throughout the Middle East. Abel Darwish and Gregory Alexander have again highlighted that:

> During the Gulf War of the 1980s the Baghdad propaganda machine, whilst promoting Iraqi nationalism, glorified the Iraqi leader as the heir of the Babylonian kings and as the leader of Pan-Arabism. This appealed to Arab nationalists--especially those amongst the Palestinians on the West Bank and in Jordan.[9]

Under his rule, Baghdad became resplendent with new roads, monuments, redevelopment zones, and 45 new shopping centers. In 1985, the ruler of Iraq erected a monument unto himself to commemorate a victory over Iran that in the end never really materialized. Saddam Hussein was present at its unveiling on the sultry afternoon of August 8, 1989, when the war against Iran ended. Thousands had gathered in the victory square. A parade began with an awesome display of military might. Loudspeakers blared with pre-recorded "Hurrahs!" The soldiers were followed by artillery, tanks, and personnel carriers pulled on long trailers and trucks. Hundreds of bright-eyed young men and women came out dressed in the national colors of Iraq; black and green and gold were everywhere. Sitting narcissistically on a white horse, in full military regalia, Saddam looked subliminally pleased with the pageantry of the occasion.

Only the simple-minded were fooled by the vainglorious art of his totalitarian order. Begun in 1985, the monument was dubbed the "Victory Arch." It consists of two sets of forearms, each weighing some 20 tons, which are much taller than the Arc de Triomphe in Paris. Each of the forearms clasps a heavy sword 40 meters high. Molded from an imprint of Saddam's own forearms, they are reproduced on a scale of 40:1, right down to the dictator's very follicles. At the base of this monument, there are nets that disgorge about 5,000 Iranian helmets, relics found not too long ago on the eastern battlegrounds.[10]

To portray Saddam as absolutely irrational is another thing that is furthest from the truth. In the opinions of many journalists, including Efraim Karsh and P. Rautsi, and Judith Miller and Laurie Mylroie, whose books in 1991 and 1990, respectively were the first serious attempts (excluding Samir al-Khalil's) to grapple with Saddam's personality, there is decidedly a consensus on irrationality in addition to ruthlessness. But there is also much evidence that points to a man possessed of cunning political savvy, an acumen for business economics--traits which are not alien to the Arabs--and an uncommon appreciation for the realities and wonders of military technology.

In medieval times the Arabs developed significant technological implements, and not only of a war-making variety: shipbuilding, the knotting of carpets, and metallurgy. But their heyday came and went; most of this technology became obsolete. The Arab world afterward fell into deep slumber. Amazingly innovative at the outset, Islam and the Islamic worldview that subsequently developed became static, excessively dogmatic, and conservative. The Prophet Mohammed had in his day preached that men should seek knowledge and wisdom as far as the four corners of the world. The Holy Koran encouraged the faithful to live by such principles. It is a pity the Arabs have today only themselves to blame for not living up to such noble standards. When their nationalist awakening came in the early twentieth century, their leaders and thinkers could point to other problems that held them back. Not all Arab intellectuals believed Arab backwardness to be the direct result of Western imperialism and colonialism.

For one thing, the Arabs were slow in mastering the language of technology the way the West has. They have been practically dominated by the West as a result of this dependence on technology. Their military technology is non-existent. And technological underdevelopment is only partly due to the poor quality of the mineral resources, the heat, and the aridity of the lands the Arabs inhabit. Their disinclination for science and technology must also be imputed to a lack of technical aptitudes; otherwise it would prove difficult to explain how well the Japanese have done in this field--and without any natural resources. What proves difficult is importing technical knowledge by a people who do not like to use it, and perhaps refuse to use it, out of feelings of disdain for manual labor.

The Arabs have been notoriously averse to heavy toil, a similarity they share with other peoples of southerly climes. The Russians, who are a northern people, have also been singled out by experts as having traits in their national character that somehow discourage the natural growth of a "work ethic" (and it does not have to be a Protestant one)--allegedly one of the causes of the Soviet Union's relative technological backwardness.[11]

For years in Iraq, as elsewhere in the modern Arab Middle East, science was something to be frowned at. Indeed, science and technology in today's age require a systemic application to the solution of ever-increasing and complex technical questions. To Arabs seeking a career opportunity, this was not considered as prestigious as more traditional worldviews and methods. The Arab schooling system placed excessive emphasis on religion, language, and literature rather than applied science or mathematics. Only clerical, mercantile, banking (although not long ago even this was discouraged in Muslim societies), and administrative opportunities were constantly sought after. Ironically, sometimes students who had received technical training--in mechanics, engineering, or computer science--would move away from these technical fields and embrace administrative, bureaucratic, or business vocations.

Like President Gorbachev, Saddam Hussein addressed this weakness in Iraq by embarking on a major reeducational effort--the whole configuration of the Arab (that is, Iraqi) national character has had to undergo a thorough modification. Unlike Gorbachev, however, Saddam was going to coerce his people to master the rudiments of modern technology, and he was going to start by inculcating his people with the artifacts of war. Saddam was farsighted enough to realize that to unify the whole Arab world, to take on a powerful Iran, to eventually challenge the West he would need a strong economy. His soldiers would have to acquire the technological skills of warfare. Oil revenues were going to help him do that. He was, in a word, out to do the very same thing for Iraq that the Iranian Shah, Mohammad Reza, had tried to do for Iran, and much more.

How realistic was the ruler of Iraq? By most accounts--shrewdly so. After the end of the second Gulf War, the government of Kuwait hired Kroll Associates, whose president, Jules Kroll, had previously traced the hidden assets of former Filipino president Ferdinand Marcos and deposed Haitian president Jean-Claude Duvalier.[12] Through careful investigation, Kroll discovered that Hussein controlled a personal fortune in excess of $10 billion, which included money he had skimmed from Iraq's oil revenues.[13] Hussein, his half brother, Barzan al-Takriti, and his son-in-law, Hussein Kamel, not only used oil profits, but demanded a 2.5 percent kickback from Japanese firms doing business in Iraq and skimmed money from contracts between the government and Saddam's own front companies. This money was invested in a number of dummy corporations and front companies so that he could buy stock in some of the best known companies in the world. Saddam was going to use his secret financial network to acquire advanced technology to upgrade Iraq's nuclear- and chemical-weapons programs and buttress its war machine. These were all realistic moves.

If Saddam Hussein, true to the despotic rulers of Iraq's past, used torture, murder, and terrorism, he was using it to a far greater degree than his predecessors. He made no friends; he surrounded himself only with agents and sycophants. He would maintain intelligence agencies that could spy on his enemies, on the army, on the people, on other Arab countries, and on each other. Like Hafez al-Assad of Syria, Saddam Hussein would not murder someone because he hated him, only because he found him dangerous. Like al-Assad, he knew when to stop before overreaching himself. Hitler, in comparison, was far more brazen, for the German leader's brinkmanship propelled him to go all the way. Saddam has demonstrated an uncanny ability to move forward and then move quickly back. His is not a brinkmanship born of despair. Mastering the ability to exaggerate, he asserts himself with bombast and flair when he knows it catches the fancy of the Arab people in both speech and personal style. But he realistically recognizes the importance of technological wherewithal when he needs to confront equal or greater powers on the battlefield. To borrow an expression from *New York Times* journalist, Thomas Friedman, Saddam Hussein and Hafez al-Assad "are always playing three-dimensional chess with the world, while Americans seem to know only how to play checkers--one plodding move at a time."[14]

On the other hand, Saddam Hussein's attitude to Israel will serve as the best illustration of the realities of Arab nationalism mixed with both imagined and contrived falsehoods and delusions about the meaning of power. For Nasser (whom Saddam always admired), Palestine might have been the nucleus of a pan-Arab state. But when Nasser was defeated in war by Israel in 1967, all hopes for a pan-Arab nationalist movement were dashed and the movement began to flag, until the ascendancy of Saddam Hussein. Saddam Hussein has been sensible enough to realize that the Arabs must not entertain too many illusions about the Palestinians. He could use them and allow himself to be used by them. The Palestinian homeland that the Zionists had usurped was part of the broader issue of pan-Arab nationalism.

The other side of the coin, however, is that Palestinians are separatists in addition to being Arab nationalists. In the short run, these two notions might be compatible when viewed as part of the common Arab struggle against the state of Israel. In the long run, they are not compatible. Most Palestinians want a homeland that is currently in Israel. The Palestine Liberation Organization (PLO) leadership has declared it wants an independent state with all the trappings of sovereignty--borders, customs, embassies, a flag, an army, and membership in the United Nations. Arab nationalists, on the other hand, who are also dubbed pan-Arabists, call for the creation of a state that will include all Arab-speaking peoples from Morocco to Oman, which would incorporate the Palestinians. Saddam has never wanted his struggle against Israel to be a struggle on behalf of the Palestinians alone. It is destined to be a righteous struggle of all Arabs, he often remarks.

For there is no real Israeli-Palestinian problem, as Saddam sees it: it has always been and will remain an Arab-Israeli conflict. Saddam is not alone in thinking this way. Palestine as a separate entity never existed when Muslims themselves ruled over this entire region from 634 to 1917. Palestine was part of a larger political unit and was never called *Palestine* by the local Arabs. In fact, the word *Palestine* was initially associated with Judaism and Christianity. In time the Muslims of this area adopted the term *Palestinian* to distinguish themselves from the Jewish (Zionist) settlers and the British rulers. But the Arabs are so divided among themselves that the Palestinian leadership had no other recourse than to splinter into a dozen fractious groupings. One is pro-Syrian, another pro-Iraqi; some are fundamentalist Islamic, one is Marxist and led by a Palestinian Christian, and so forth. Yasser Arafat is not the only Palestinian leader; and at one point, in the early 1970s, there was bad blood between Arafat's PLO and Jordan's King Hussein. Furthermore, without the funding from non-Palestinians, especially the Gulf states, the Palestinian movement would be nowhere. And there are so many Palestinians living in the Gulf coastal states that it would not matter to the Palestinians if Iraq dominated the Gulf as long as Iraq supported the Palestinian cause, even if it were to the detriment of the Gulf states.

In order to help the Palestinian cause of liberation, all the Arab governments in the Middle East, including Kuwait and Saudi Arabia, have subtly and insidiously belabored the theme of the Zionist and the Jew as the embodiment of evil, the ultimate bogeyman, a malignant growth that must be extirpated. All Arab countries, just like czarist Russia and Nazi Germany, have for the past four decades been teaching Arab children about the blood libel, the accusation that the Jews used the blood of non-Jewish children for religious purposes, usually on the Hebrew Passover. Iraq is not alone among the Arab states in charging the Jews with having corrupted the pure Muslim and Christian society in Palestine by bringing death, destruction, and prostitution to the country. Arab officials have done their utmost in borrowing from old Muslim literature, ancient folklore sung by poets like Mohi Aldin bin Arabi,[15] and drawing on all the well-worn Western Christian fabrications to charge the Jews with being the eternal enemies of humanity and responsible for two world wars.

More than this, to date there have been no fewer than 12 Arab translations of the full text of the "Protocols of the Elders of Zion." The Protocols provided the ideological justification that ultimately and logically led to the

"Final Solution" of the gas chambers during the reign of the Third Reich in Europe. The Protocols, like other writings on the same theme, tell the story of the blood libels of history and preposterously detail a conspiracy by world Jewry. Once Abdel Nasser called the Protocols to the attention of a visiting Indian writer, indicating that they "proved beyond any shadow of doubt that three hundred Zionists control the destinies of Europe."[16] The new generation of Iraqis have been brought up to hate, despise, and fear the Israelis. Israel has for decades been slated for annihilation[17] and no self-respecting Iraqi, if he wishes to survive, could contradict the dissemination of such ideas by his government. With the exception of Egypt, most Arab governments follow the same line of propaganda.[18] Indeed, very few Arab intellectuals, even abroad, express contradictory opinions.

Saddam Hussein and the Iraqi state have not recognized Israel; they have never had any serious intentions about negotiating with Israel and have considered themselves in a state of war with Israel since 1948.

NOTES

1.   Judith Miller and Laurie Mylroie, *Saddam Hussein and the Crisis in the Gulf* (New York: Times Books, 1990), p. 34.

2.   Samir al-Khalil, *Republic of Fear: The Politics of Modern Iraq* (Berkeley: University of California Press, 1989), p. 110.

3.   Marion Farouk-Sluglett and Peter Sluglett, *Iraq Since 1958: From Revolution to Dictatorship* (London: KPI, 1987), pp. 207-208.

4.   Abel Darwish and Gregory Alexander, *Unholy Babylon* (London: Victor Gollancz Ltd., 1991), p. 220.

5.   See al-Khalil, *Republic of Fear*, p. 219.

6.   *Newsweek*, March 11, 1991, p. 17.

7.   Quoted in al-Khalil, *Republic of Fear*, p. 122.

8.   Darwish and Alexander, *Unholy Babylon*, p. 197.

9.   Ibid., p. 14.

10.   See Samir al-Khalil, *The Monument* (Berkeley: University of California Press, and London: André Deutsch, 1991).

11.   See, for example, Marshall Goldman, *Gorbachev's Challenge: Economic Reform in the Age of High Technology* (New York: Norton, 1987). Zbigniew Brzezinski, President Carter's security advisor, once stated that "Russians are not Prussians."

12.   John Greenwald, "Did Saddam Skim Billions?," *Time*, April 8, 1991, p. 46.

13.   Ibid.

14.   Thomas Friedman, *From Beirut to Jerusalem* (New York: Doubleday, 1989), p. 103.

15.   See the prologue in this book.

16. R. K. Karanjia, *The Arab Dawn* (Bombay, 1958), p. 330.

17. Habib Bourguiba, one-time president of Tunisia, did, however, suggest that the Arabs should recognize Israel.

18. Henry Cattan, in *The Palestine Question* (London, Sydney: Croom Helm, 1989) offers a view from the Arab side. He writes: "As part of the process of obliterating Palestinian history and culture, the history of Palestine is not taught in Israeli schools." (p. 216).

3

"Qadissiyat Saddam"

If one were to sum up Saddam's political state of mind throughout the 1970s, it would reveal five specific problems that he intended to resolve: the competition with Iran for regional power; the Palestinian question; the threat of Israel, which is linked to the Palestinian issue; the long-standing claim of Iraq on Kuwait; and the Kurds of northern Iraq.

With Iraq's newly revamped Revolutionary Command Council and army, which was receiving the lion's share of the budget from the country's burgeoning oil revenues, Saddam was ready to embark on an ambitious path to glory. It came roughly at the same time that Iran was undergoing a social revolution and ridding the nation of its Pahlavi monarchy.

In the Gulf region, two main powers have always asserted themselves: Iran and Iraq. The eight-year war that erupted between these two countries in September 1980 came as no real surprise given the history and the personalities of its leaders.

Iraq is a Sunni-ruled nation where the majority are Shi'a Arabs. Iran is officially Shi'a. There is an affinity between the Shi'ites of Iran and the Shi'ites of Iraq. Khomeini's ideology was a fundamentalist, millenarian ideology of Ithna 'Ashari Shi'ism. This ideology is the foundation upon which Khomeini built his doctrine of *vilayat-i faqih* ("the governance of the jurisprudent): a doctrine enshrined in the new constitution of the Islamic Republic of Iran. Khomeini declared that the concept of *vilayat-i faqih* had universal application. This meant that Khomeini's ideology could be exported to all other Muslim countries that refused to accept Imam Khomeini as their spiritual leader. Khomeini often referred to Saddam Hussein as Yazid, the murderer of Hussein (one of the central martyrs in Shi'a Islam). Also, the Iraqis, for the most part (with the exception of a sizable Christian and Kurdish minority), are Arabs while the Iranians are Persian.

A further bone of contention is territorial: Iraq has traditionally laid claim to the whole of the Shatt-al-Arab River estuary. This waterway was to play an important role in Saddam's relations with the Shah's government and with Khomeini's regime. The 1975 Algiers Agreement stipulated that the boundary was to run along the middle of the river, where the water is deepest. In 1975, Iran possessed a superb army and navy; it was the most powerful country in the Middle East, an important Organization of Petroleum Exporting Countries (OPEC) negotiator, and a bulwark of stability in the region, the United States's putative "policeman" in the Persian Gulf. Iraq had to acknowledge this fact and behave accordingly. But the last point of the 1975 agreement was that the Shah would no longer help the Iraqi Kurds militarily and deny the Kurds access to Iran. The resulting peace with Iran, drafted behind the backs of the Kurds, allowed Saddam Hussein to strengthen his power base.

Having become the undisputed leader of Iraq in 1979, the Iraqi president carefully took time out to observe what the Ayatollah Khomeini was up to when the Iranian ecclesiastic also consolidated his power in the same year. Saddam must have watched with particular glee as the Shah went down to defeat and went off to an undignified exile and premature death. He watched and waited as the Iranian army was being pilloried by the Islamic Revolution and then indiscriminately purged of its best officers and pilots while radical religious leaders came to power. He must have reacted with some horror, too, as he realized the potential of the new fundamentalism that was sweeping across the entire Middle East. Radical fundamentalism could easily cost him his own power inside Iraq. The Shi'a Muslims were, after all, in a slight majority in Iraq. No sooner was Khomeini sitting snugly in power than he made it known how much he hoped that Iraq would also become an Islamic republic.

As Saddam pondered over this, he came to the dawning realization that war with Iran could not be avoided if Iraq were to go ahead and decisively assert itself as the sole leader of the Arab world and the only power--barring none--in the (he would never call it the "Persian") Arab Gulf. Saddam would make no secret of coveting the rich oil-bearing region of Iran called Khuzistan, where primarily ethnic Arabs lived and which most Arabs considered to be the ancestral Arab lands of "Arabistan" anyway. The three little islands that the Shah had seized in the Strait of Hormuz in the mid-1970s (the two Tumbs and Abu Musa) were also supposed to be an integral part of Iraq. The regime in Teheran, moreover, was in its infancy, so that the time of the attack on Iran could not be delayed any longer. Baghdad also made no secret about stopping the spread of fundamentalism throughout the Gulf region and holding Iraq's indigenous Shi'a population from becoming contaminated by the Iranian virus. Saddam was going to catch the Iranians in the middle of their revolutionary spree. He reasoned that the Arabs of Khuzistan would rise to the occasion against the Iranians. So too would the Iranian Kurds. Earlier in the year, 52

Americans had been taken hostage in their embassy, and relations between the United States and Iran had entered a period of unprecedented
acrimony.

Baghdad possessed enough military intelligence to conclude that the
sterling Iranian military machine had been irreparably weakened by
revolutionary purges. The future was to prove that Saddam Hussein had
miscalculated the options and outcomes and had underestimated the
Iranians. He especially miscalculated the support he hoped he would get
from the ethnic Arabs living in Khuzistan. He was wrong, too, about his
own offensive capabilities. When the Iraqi army invaded Iranian Khuzistan,
preceded by a massive though largely ineffectual aerial bombardment,
eight years of bloody war ensued. It was a murderous war, exceeding in
casualties--about one million--the Arab-Israeli wars combined, if one had
to make a comparison with other Mideast wars fought until then. To
Saddam, to the whole Iraqi people, it came to be known as "*Qadissiyat
Saddam*"--Saddam's Qadissiya, or Saddam's and the Arabs' modern-day
victory over the Persians.

The date September 17, 1980, is cherished as a particular milestone
in the history of Iraq. For about a month before that date the two countries
had been skirmishing across the border with artillery and small-arms fire.
One month after the fighting began, Saddam stood before the National
Assembly, now a legislative body little more than his rubber stamp. In a
voice reminiscent of the histrionics of Egyptian president Gamal Abdel
Nasser (who had announced the nationalization of the Suez Canal in
1956), Saddam Hussein abrogated the March 6, 1975, agreement with
Iran. He solemnly called "for the return of the 'Iraqi-Arab Shatt-al-Arab' with
full rights and sovereignty." On the 22nd, without a declaration of war, Iraq
invaded Iran across the Shatt and pushed into Khuzistan Province in a
matter of days, seizing and annexing 1,000 square kilometers.

Once the Iraqis invaded and annexed Iran's oil-rich province of Khuzistan, all the former Iranian cities were renamed in Arabic: Khuzistan
became Arabistan, and so forth. Iraqi administration, law, and currency
were extended to the areas held by the Iraqis. Depriving Iran of its major
oil fields would easily have ended any future attempts by Iran to restore its
power in the Gulf.

The Iraqi forces penetrated northwestern Iran, coming within 50 miles
of Sanandaj in Iranian Kurdistan. Having suppressed a Kurdish insurrection
in their own country, the Iraqis now began supporting Iranian Kurds in their
struggle against the Khomeini government.

Almost immediately, the Gulf Arab countries backed Iraq and
promised Hussein volunteers and money. Iraq projected the image of a
moderate, in contrast to its extremist and bellicose neighbor. It also saw
itself as the defender of the Arab world against the anti-Arab Islamic
pretender of the Iranian government. Saddam was happiest when he could

bask in this image. It made for excellent propaganda among the Arab masses. He could play on the theme of being the true heir of the great Egyptian leader, Gamal Nasser. Saddam did not hesitate to capitalize on this image by demanding money from the other Gulf Arab states who needed protection against the Persian bogeyman. Iran was thus virtually isolated in the world community; it could only be supported by other international pariahs such as Libya, Syria, and Algeria and, to some extent, far-away North Korea, while almost all the Western nations were quick to sympathize with Iraq.

To the impartial observer it seemed that the Iranians were bound to be utterly defeated. The ayatollah's armed forces lacked adequate air power and were ill-equipped; the commanders in the regular army were incompetent; and Iranian clerics were taking matters into their own hands, deciding military-related issues and indoctrinating officers and men alike. Saddam was expecting a resounding victory--perhaps a short battle engagement, but nothing short of a rout.

When fighting erupted, the Iranians suffered untold casualties from Iraqi artillery fire; Iranian infantry smarted from the initial drubbing. But the Iraqi forces failed to take into account the revolutionary fervor then gripping the Iranian population. Khomeini himself had galvanized the Iranian soldiers, turning them literally into cannon fodder, exhorting them, if that proved necessary, to become martyrs in the defense of Iran. By late October, the Iranians had slowed the Iraqi invasion to a crawl. The Iraqi military command was surprised but not unprepared. By January of 1981 the Iranians launched a counteroffensive near Susangerd, which the Iraqi defenders easily, albeit temporarily, defeated.

Iraq was militarily superior by a 5 to 1 margin (which in time rose to 10 to 1) with far better logistics, although Iraq's population in 1980 was 15 million and Iran's was 45 million. The Iraqis' operational doctrine for offense and defense was based on the Soviet model of warfare taught them by Russian advisors. But the Iraqi commanders were taking orders from Saddam alone, who had already become the commander in chief. The Iraqi generals themselves could not implement offensive actions in the Soviet manner, involving a lightning war with large tank formations. Iraqi officers and NCOs showed little initiative on the offense, waiting too long for higher headquarters to provide direction. Defensively, however, they were superb. In the early days of the war, before the improvements came in, Iraqi defenses can best be described as Aaron Danis did in the U.S. Army review, *Military Intelligence.*

> Iraqi defenses usually consisted of three dug-in defensive bands, about 8 kilometers wide and 10 kilometers deep for an infantry or mechanized division sector, with an 8 kilometer deep forward security zone manned by the divisional reconnaissance battalion.

Divisions deployed two brigades forward, and each of the brigade sectors had battalion triangle-shaped strong points. These provided all-around protection through the use of alternate firing positions and dug-in armor positions which obscured tanks to full defilade. Strong points had interlocking fire and they were covered by massed artillery and CAS, due to Iraq's air superiority throughout the Iran-Iraq War.[1]

In the spring of 1981, Iran unveiled its "human-wave" attacks, with major offensives following in March and May 1982. Despite Iraq's technological mobility and firepower advantages, the human-wave assaults nearly overwhelmed the Iraqi defenders. Yet the more competent Iraqi commanders fared not much better than the Iranians, and both sides were dismally deficient in offensive tank warfare. Most of the Iranian losses occurred when their tanks mired in the sand, were poorly maintained, or were abandoned.

In March 1982, Iranian forces rolled the Iraqis back west of Dezful and forced Saddam's defenses back across the border; by May, the Iranian infantry offensives recaptured most of Khuzistan, including the port of Khorramshahr, and by July the Iranians were approaching the very gates of Basra, Iraq's Shi'a metropolis and second largest city, near the northern tip of the Shatt-al-Arab. The only reason the Iranians were able to do so well in these attacks was because they had huge manpower resources-- the Iranians were operating like a steamroller.

The Iranian plan was to take Basra and to cut the road to Baghdad, before making a final assault on the Iraqi capital. Lacking modern weapons--mainly tanks, artillery, and aircraft--they could not make any use of a combined forces operation. The casualties among the Iranians were enormous. Draft dodging was widespread. The army's morale began to sag. Every offensive the Iranians launched ended up as a "mini-jihad." The mullahs, or religious leaders, interfered in military decisions every inch of the way. They and the Pasdaran, or Revolutionary Guard, undermined the professionalism of the regular army by believing in a divine mandate, fighting with religious fervor rather than carefully planning their tactics. While the Iranians were able to dislodge the Iraqis by using the Pasdaran as shock troops and the Baseej (untrained paramilitary forces taking the initial shock of the human-wave assaults), they lapsed into a World War I-style offensive leading to heavy casualties and little gains. For the next five years the war entered a stalemate.

Iraq was able to hold Khomeini's soldiers by using mustard gas in 1982-83 to disrupt the human-wave assaults. Baghdad had at its disposal massive air support, including Mi-25 and French-built Gazelle attack helicopters. Iraqi defensive lines were well maintained. When the General Staff appeared to be overwhelmed by the sheer numbers of the attackers,

Iraq resorted to Tabun and Sarin nerve gases and cyanotic agents. The chemicals were used more as a terror weapon, wreaking panic in the Iranian ranks. But the Iranians soon developed countermeasures, and chemical agents were, in any case, only effective when the winds were favorable.

On the whole the Iranians were suffering more in material damages than the Iraqis. Teheran could buy virtually nothing abroad on credit. When the oil refinery at Tabriz was raided in a single afternoon with incendiary bombs, the Iraqis were able to wipe out one-quarter of Iran's internal oil supply. Iranian oil exports had fallen to 800,000 barrels per day from 1,300,000. In the winters, Iran was running low on benzene,[2] food was rationed. Morale and the mood in Iran were also dismally low. By contrast, Iraq's capital exuded an artificial calm. There was popular resentment against the war, especially by Iraqi Shi'ites, but living standards were kept high. Money was coming in from the Gulf Arab states. Baghdad's streets were extraordinarily peaceful, eerily peaceful; meat and fruits and vegetables and heating oil were plentiful. Saddam's regime played up the news of volunteers coming from other Arab countries to enlist in the army and air force. Yasser Arafat was a frequent visitor to the Iraqi capital, and thousands of Palestinians came to help in the war effort, abandoning any initial ties they had made with the Iranians.

In the first years of conflict the war was largely ignored by the world. Neither side invited foreign journalists to the killing fields. The U.S. government and the other Western countries more or less expected the belligerents to neutralize each other. Although Teheran had received a small number of tanks, spare parts, and Silkworm missiles from China, no one else would sell weapons to Iran.[3] Attempts to impose sanctions and arms embargoes were directed mainly against Khomeini, rather than the original aggressor, Iraq. The Americans, in fact, delayed a meeting of the U.N. Security Council and any condemnation of Iraq. Feelings in the West and general public opinion were overwhelmingly in favor of Iraq. Western politicians only saw Shi'a fundamentalism as a potentially destabilizing factor. Saddam Hussein, the real aggressor, was now being perceived as the victim of aggression, yet he was singled out as the only promise, the only potential bulwark against Khomeini's fanaticism.

To be sure, the U.N. Security Council did adopt Resolution 579, which called for a ceasefire. But it did not condemn Iraq for the invasion. Suddenly, in February of 1986, Iran launched a two-pronged offensive on the Basra front. The northern prong was meant as a diversion and had the effect of successfully keeping the Iraqis bogged down with the defense of Basra. The southern thrust was aimed against the Fao Peninsula, on Iraq's Gulf coast. The Iranians moved under the cover of darkness. Heavy rains and cloud cover blanketed the whole Shatt-al-Arab in a dense fog. Iranian infantrymen and Pasdaran made an amphibious landing on the other side of the Shatt and surprised the poorly prepared Iraqi defenses by capturing the abandoned port of Al Fao. The Iraqis very quickly counterattacked but were driven back. The loss of the peninsula was a tremendous blow to President Hussein. He had to regain the initiative before the Iranians spearheaded another movement to capture Basra and Baghdad.

Ending the war was out of the question for Hussein; he certainly could not make a gesture that might be construed as weakness by the Iranians. Iraq indeed would only accept a peace plan that "left the Takritis, the Sunni elite, the Revolutionary Command Council, the Ba'ath and Iraq, in that order, intact."[4] That was the whole impasse. But come what may, Saddam still had the sympathy and support of the West working for him.

Only the Soviet Union appeared to draw closer to Iran as the war progressed. While Iran considered the Soviet Union to be one of the Great Satans, the USSR was still the enemy of the United States: "the enemy of my enemy is my friend" was how Teheran reasoned. Moscow and Teheran soon found themselves signing the first in a number of agreements respecting pipeline and oil transit routes.

For their part, the Americans were interested in preventing any Soviet influence or military presence in the Gulf area. They thus joined with Great Britain, France, Belgium, Holland, and Italy to protect shipping interests in the Persian Gulf by escorting a number of reflagged oil tankers through the mined corridors of the Gulf. By January of 1988, however, a number of the European countries agreed to cut back the number of minesweepers that they had deployed in the area.[5]

Western nations were especially concerned about the disruption of oil flow from the Gulf, which would jeopardize the West's political, military, and economic freedom of action. Western capitals were already casting about for a contingency plan, and ways were found to circumvent this problem. The protection of oil tankers in the Gulf (especially through the Strait of Hormuz between Iran and the United Arab Emirates) was one solution. Another involved the building of pipelines. In 1987, the International Energy Agency reported that the Gulf countries exported about nine million barrels of oil per day, seven million of it by sea, which supplied a third of the oil imported by the 24 "Organization for Economic Cooperation and Development" countries, including the United States and Canada, most Western European countries, and Japan, and furnished nearly a fifth of the world's total consumption.[6]

The 1986 winter breakthrough at Fao caused more than just a few shivers running down the spine of the Iraqi military command. The generals began grumbling about Saddam's interference. As casualties began to mount, every day news was reported of soldiers missing in action--they were dead or presumed dead; many had been taken prisoner and transported to Iran. Support for the Iraqi cause appeared to be lackluster. Analysts and reporters, commentators and academics were predicting that the Iranian victory was only a matter of time. Khomeini himself declared that the "road to Jerusalem passes through Baghdad."[7] One Western analyst observed, somewhat shortsightedly: "Iraqi military leadership borders on the incompetent, and Iraqi troops, especially infantry, have little motivation."[8] A cliché had gained wide currency that said that "Iran cannot lose the war and Iraq cannot win it," the implication being that time was on Iran's side.

But that was not to be. Saddam had decided to let his generals have a free hand in the running of military operations. The war had now degenerated into a conflict of attrition. What everyone failed to realize was that Iraq's position was beginning to improve from year to year. In pure military expenditures Iraq consistently outspent Iran (which could not buy anything on credit), buying approximately 12 billion dollars' worth of military-related supplies and materials, including the hiring of technicians to build reinforced bunkers, backup communications systems, and chemicals. As the war continued into 1987, Iraq gained access to quality arms supplies. The Iraqi army actually grew fivefold, with superiority in tanks and artillery. The Iranian commander of the Revolutionary Guard, Mohsen Reza'i, was to lament after the war:

> They had armour and we did not. If our circumstances in the war are not taken into account when comparisons are made with classical warfare, it will be a major error on the part of the analysts. We were unarmed infantrymen against the enemy's cavalry. There are few instances in the history of Islam of such a war.[9]

While Iran's manpower fell by early 1988 by 100,000,[10] Saddam Hussein was boasting that "our people, who began with 12 divisions at the beginning of the war, now have about 70 divisions at the end of the war. The entire world has never seen such a development."[11]

However, by 1988 the Gulf countries could move about half of their exports by pipeline and new pipelines were under construction. Both Iran and Iraq were dependent upon oil; its sale accounted for about 90 percent of their foreign exchange.[12] Iraq had been able to restore its oil trade by shipping its oil through pipelines. Iran had always shipped by sea and was concerned about Iraqi attacks on its shipping during the conflict.

Abel Darwish and Gregory Alexander, in their 1991 book, *Unholy Babylon*, argued that Iraq was desperately trying to end the war on its own terms. Baghdad built up a $100 billion debt while Iran had borrowed only a minimal amount that they could easily service.[13] About $30 billion was owed by Iraq to Kuwait alone. Baghdad set about manipulating international events, and it is said that Saddam Hussein caused the Israelis to invade Lebanon when Iraqi agents hired the Abu Nidal group in 1982 to

assassinate the Israeli ambassador to Britain, Shlomo Argov. Some
observers have been suggesting that Israel blamed the PLO for the assassination and then invaded Beirut as a result. Iraq then tried to end the war
with Iran by saying they had to finish the war in view of "the urgent
necessity of directing all efforts towards confronting the ferocious Zionist
aggression against the Arab world, the Palestinian people and
Lebanon."[14]

THE NORTHERN FRONT

The Gulf was not the only theater of battle. There was a northern front
as well: the so-called Kurdish front, which the world would have forgotten
had it not been for a monstrous crime committed there in 1988. That crime
beggars description; we shall come to it in due course.

In the summer of 1983, with Iran thrusting into northern Iraq, the
Barzanis (the major Kurdish tribe under Mullah Mustafa Barzani)[15] spearheading the drive, the Iranian Kurds were impaled on the horns of a
dilemma: were they to ally themselves with the Iranians, joining forces with
the villainous Barzanis, something they would never have done before?
Or were they to assist Saddam Hussein? Saddam Hussein set about re-
newing his offer of limited autonomy in return for Kurdish support in
defending northern Iraq against the Iranians. In January 1984, there was
an exchange of prisoners between Iranian Kurds and Baghdad. Iranian
Kurdish units were henceforth incorporated into the Regular Iraqi Army as
border guards. The war in the north had become a war of proxies, both
sides depending heavily on Kurdish surrogate forces--Iraq on Talabani and
Ghassemlou, Iran on the Barzanis.[16] Once again, a balance in the power
game was being played out, with the Kurds as both pawns and manipu-
lators. The Saddam-Talabani arrangement--I should point out that Arabs
and Kurds and Turks have always made strange bedfellows--was most
discomforting to Turkey.

The American military analyst Stephen C. Pelletiere was one of the
first writers who warned the West about the Kurds. He argued that "with
a Kurdish population of over 5 million in eastern Anatolia (adjacent to Iraqi
Kurdistan) the Turks feared the effect of Iraq's offer of semi-autonomy to
the Kurds."[17] Faced with an active Kurdish separatist movement on their
territory, "the Turks," concluded Pelletiere, "could reasonably complain to
both Iran and Iraq that by arming the Kurds, they risk destabilizing the
whole Turkish-Iraq-Iran triangle."[18]

In December 1986, at the height of the Iran-Iraq war, a three-day
conference was held in Teheran under the rallying motif "Cooperation
Conference of the Iraqi Peoples." The conference gathered together
diverse Iraqi groups whose only shared attribute was their opposition to the
Ba'ath regime. One of the main objectives of the three-day conference was

to bring together the two main factions of the Iraqi opposition and the Islamic movement. Many secular politicians also participated, including ex-monarchists, ex-Ba'athists, Christians, and distinguished Iraqi personalities.[19] Only the Iraqi Communists did not show up. The conference was addressed by the Iranian president, Ali Khamenei, as well as Prime Minister Hossein Mousavi, the speaker of the Iranian Parliament, Hashemi Rafsanjani, and Foreign Minister Ali Akbar Velayati. "President Khamenei confirmed Iran's commitment to an independent and free Iraq within its recognized international borders--a clear warning that Iran would not hesitate to challenge any intervention by other countries in the affairs of Iraq."[20] The message was obviously aimed at Turkey, a neighboring country and a member of NATO.

Turkey's historical claims to the Mosul and Kirkuk area had been the focus of persistent attention. Iqbal Asaria noted that Turkey has periodically expressed its claim to northern Iraq, an area that used to be the "*vilayet*" of Mosul under the Ottoman Empire.[21] He further argued that Turkey's dependence on the oil pipeline from Kirkuk and the possible impact of any change on its large but suppressed Kurdish population might be used as an excuse if and when both the United States and Turkey ever sought to dismember Iraq. At a time when the Gulf War was going well for Iran, the Khomeini leadership sent clear signals that it would not countenance any such move on the part of Turkey.[22] In a related theme, Zubaida Umar argued that Turkey had not done much to espouse the cause of the Turkomans in the Kirkuk area, estimated to be around one million. However, "as Saddam Hussein nears the end of his tether [it was wishful thinking to say such a thing at the time], the [Turks] might use them as a pretext for intervention,"[23] Umar added. We must remember that he was writing at a moment when he believed that the Iranians would capture Basra. But the Ba'athist regime in Baghdad successfully withstood every Iranian onslaught. Baghdad did not fall.

Faced with the likelihood of an Iranian victory spilling over into the friendly Arab states of the Gulf, U.S. officials began to take better stock of the situation. Moreover, the leaders of the six-nation Gulf Cooperation Council (GCC), which met in Riyadh in early January 1988, decided to coordinate their defense strategies and appealed to the Americans for help. There was an all-out panic in the Gulf when Iran began launching Chinese-built Silkworm missiles against Kuwait, a member of the GCC. At the GCC summit, King Fahd of Saudi Arabia reportedly said that the Iranians "were pointing their arrows to our chests instead of helping us to liberate Jerusalem from Zionist domination. There is no reasonable justification for this other than the desire for expansion."[24] The situation was becoming so serious that the GCC raised the possibility of direct Egyptian military assistance in the wake of a new solidarity between Egypt and the Arab states.[25]

It seemed that the whole world was ostracizing Iran for not complying with U.N. Resolution 598, which called upon the belligerents to agree to a ceasefire. In late December 1987, all the members of the U.N. Security Council, including China and the Soviet Union, signed a statement saying they would impose an arms embargo if Iran did not comply. Work on a draft of the actual embargo resolution was expected to begin in late January 1988. But that never got anywhere; resolutions are only pieces of paper, and Iran was not fooled. Behind the scenes, the Soviet Union, making a bid to get into the act, issued a proposal to the Reagan administration according to which both the Soviets and the Americans would enforce the embargo under U.N. auspices, primarily by blockading the entire Gulf region. The White House rejected the idea on the grounds that it involved an increased Soviet presence in the Gulf, thus possibly threatening U.S. interests. For their part, the Arabs would still have preferred stationing Egyptian troops, but Egypt, short of helping the Iraqis with pilot training, refused to have anything to do with the Gulf.[26]

It was at this point, in February 1988, that the U.S. government, without making the issue formal and public, decided to throw in its lot with Iraq. On several occasions in the 1980s, Saddam had expressed his interest in expanding diplomatic contacts with the United States. The Reagan administration at last responded positively to these overtures, and in 1984 diplomatic relations were reestablished. Iraq was then immediately removed from the list of countries accused of aiding and abetting terrorism and without further ado, such as criticisms within Congress, all U.S. restrictions on exports to Iraq were lifted. In fact, when the existence of Iraq as a state was at risk, Saddam Hussein made every effort to emphasize to the U.S. government the value of his regime's survival. France, too, had been supporting the Iraqi war effort with Etendard fighter planes, so it had an abiding interest in preventing an Iraqi military defeat. But it was the United States that was becoming Iraq's protector. By 1984, Iraq was receiving intelligence information from U.S. satellites passing over the battlefronts and from Saudi Arabian AWACs.[27] It was precisely this satellite reconnaissance information from the United States that helped the Iraqis bring the war to a successful conclusion.

BAGHDAD LAUNCHES OPERATION "BLESSED RAMADAN"

Feeling emboldened, and with Egyptian backing (as well as Saudi and Kuwaiti financing), Saddam Hussein decided that Iraq should finally move to the offensive in early 1988. A conference debating this subject was actually held in Baghdad.[28] At the end of February, Iraqi foreign minister Tariq Aziz asked the United States to delay any diplomatic action designed to impose an arms embargo. Iraq then began pressing its "war of the cities" with constant missile barrages lasting from late February until mid-

April. The demonstrated superiority in missile stockpiles during the last round of this exchange paid off for Iraq inasmuch as Iran stopped its own missile attacks on Baghdad and gave up the long-range artillery attacks against Basra, the strategic Iraqi city in the south that Iran had failed to capture in 1987 after several human-wave offensives that cost more than 80,000 lives.

The next step in the Iraqi strategic plan was to launch a series of attacks in order to regain all the territory occupied by Iran. But this could not have been accomplished without careful military planning in logistics and intelligence gathering, thus suggesting that Iraq could not have brought off its startling victories if the United States had not provided the Iraqi army with the necessary satellite intelligence that helped turn the tide against attacking Iranian forces.

By 1987, Iraq realized that its entire army needed to be retrained if it was going to perform as an offensive military machine. A new manpower pool had to be opened that previously did not exist, and that pool had to come from Iraq's student population. Unlike Iran, throughout the war the Ba'athists interdicted all able-bodied men to travel overseas, and students from wealthy families, who normally would have gone abroad to study, remained in the country. The trick now was to induct this pool of middle-class youth into the armed forces. Young men who had not been students for years now were rounded up by press gangs and dragged off the streets. But with the students more care was needed; they were brighter, more technically inclined, easier to teach, and particularly useful in the Republican Guard. It was the first time that Saddam Hussein was going to accept students into the Guard. Prior to this, only young men from the environs of Takrit were permitted to serve in its privileged ranks.

At the start of the war, the Guard had been Saddam's personal bodyguard. It then became an elite unit, performing tasks the regular army had difficulties with. In 1988, it had already become the Iraqi army's offensive/counteroffensive arm,[29] though not like Napoleon's Guards' regiments, more like Hitler's elite Waffen SS. When the Iraqis first lost the Fao Peninsula, they possessed only three Republican Guard brigades. On the eve of the counteroffensive in April 1988, this number had mushroomed to 25.

The students did not just join such an elite force; they eagerly volunteered. The Iraqi military needed aggressive spirits: draftees would not do, for they were pressured to serve. The Guard paid better. The training was more rigorous, but its members enjoyed social and economic privileges and freedoms in a society that was otherwise run as a police state. The Guards were primarily trained in the art of offensive tactics, as counterattack units, and in combined arms and maneuver operations. The force acquired its own artillery and helicopter support and trained in armor and in special-forces operations. They were the only units receiving the formidable Soviet T-72 tanks and in the impending assault were led by the best military man in the entire armed forces: Major General Iyad Khalifa Al-Rawi.[30]

After this beefing up, the Republican Guard numbered approximately 100,000. Together with the VII Corps of the regular army, another 100,000 battle-hardened soldiers, it set out to stage several dress rehearsals in preparation for the ultimate reoccupation of the Fao Peninsula. The practice sessions were conducted throughout 1987, during lulls in the fighting, over terrain similar to Fao.

Saddam Hussein charged Lieutenant General Maher al-Rashid with the entire operation. A vivacious, flamboyant soldier, al-Rashid had commanded the VII Corps on the Basra front since 1986 and had gained valuable experience against the Iranians. Al-Rashid was every bit a professional; he was probably the best strategist the Iraqis had, one who could combine Soviet military tactics with British concepts and training. His uncle, Abdullah al-Rashid, a Takriti like the whole al-Rashid family, had been bludgeoned to death in cold blood many years earlier by the teenage Saddam, a crime that had been planned to the last detail by Saddam's uncle, Khairallah Tulfah. Twenty-eight years later, the nephew, General Maher al-Rashid, took his revenge in a very subtle Takriti fashion. While on a visit to front-line positions during the war, Saddam Hussein and his bodyguards were caught in a pocket and ran the risk of falling into the hands of advancing Iranian troops. As the Iranians counterattacked, al-Rashid saved the situation in the nick of time--but he made Saddam request the assistance by swearing "*Bihyiat Abdallah al-Rashid*," the name of the general's murdered uncle. Saddam did so but resented it for a long time.

Al-Rashid now needed to plan the recapture of Fao before the onset of the sweltering heat of the summer months. He even gave the offensive a subtle code name: "Blessed Ramadan," so called to surprise the Iranian defense with a final blow as the Iranians fasted during the start of Ramadan. For their part, the Iranians were supported with heavy artillery, but they had no armor, no tank barriers, no depth, nor any air support. Most Iranian infantrymen were conscripts, with little training for mechanized warfare and gas attacks. Holy Ramadan was scheduled to come at the end of April in 1988. Temperatures between May and September were expected to rise well above 100 degrees Fahrenheit. The battlefield at Fao was flat and swampy, interspersed with numerous little lakes; the marshland and bogs made it a nightmare for anything but infantry combat. The March rains had pelted the ground so hard the marshes nearly turned to quicksand. Booby traps, barbed wire, and mine fields ringed the Iranian defenses.

General al-Rashid planned a two-pronged, three-phased operation calculated to last anywhere from four to five days, by which time he expected the Iranians to be thoroughly routed. The Iraqis used a diversionary tactic by pretending to mass huge forces in the north, in Kurdistan, which was the traditional Iranian invasion route. Saddam Hussein and his defense minister made highly publicized visits to this front in Kurdistan; every impression was given that large forces were moving north.[31] The Iraqi ground attack aimed at regaining the Fao Peninsula coincided with the heaviest fighting between U.S. naval forces and Iran in the Gulf.

The Iranians were so preoccupied with the U.S. Navy in an area stretching twenty kilometers along their coastline that they did not expect the Iraqi attack to come so soon and so suddenly. Their manpower at Fao was down to 15,000 men, all fresh conscripts and poorly supplied by makeshift pontoon bridges across the Shatt. General al-Rashid began the attack in the predawn hours of April 17, from positions ten miles north of the abandoned part of Al Fao. First there was a one-hour artillery barrage. Then Baghdad's fighter bombers and helicopters flew over 300 sorties. Since the Iraqis outnumbered the Iranian defenders 20 to 1, there was no need to use any chemical weapons. The Iranians were so surprised by the swiftness of the attack, coinciding as it did with their simultaneous skirmishing with the American navy in the Gulf, that they believed it was the Americans who were manning the Iraqi helicopter gunships in the attack on Fao--so effective was the use of helicopters and diversion.

Republican Guard units stealthily deployed special forces to cut holes through the barbed wire and mine fields prior to the attack they now called "*Tawakalna ala Allah.*" While al-Rashid's VII Corps pushed headlong through palm groves parallel to the Shatt, the Republican Guards moved southeast from positions between Zubair and Umm Qasr, then through the Great Salt Lake, a tidal swamp west of Al Fao, "often wading through chest-high water barriers."[32] With these two pincer movements, elements of the Guards also made amphibious landings behind the Iranian lines, skillfully executing a minute and dangerous commando operation.

By noon of April 18, it was all over. The Iranian troops panicked and retreated back across the Shatt waterway. Casualties were surprisingly light on both sides. The rout had been complete. General al-Rashid had made but one forgivable mistake--the battle for Al Fao did not last more than 36 hours.

The flight of the Iranian troops caused no sensation in the Iraqi military command. There was no ripple effect in Baghdad's civilian population; no propaganda over the city's airwaves. There was no attempt to pursue the Iranians across the east bank of the Shatt. The Iraqis proceeded to mop up and invited representatives of the world press to report on the event.

The next phase of General al-Rashid's plan came one month later, attacking the Iranians farther north along the border at Fish Lake, east of Basra near Shalamcheh. It came at 0930 on May 25, 1988, a time when the weather was extremely hot and the ground dry enough to commit more than a thousand tanks. Al-Rashid wanted to keep his casualties as low as possible. He did. Even Iranian casualties were very low, numbering only a few hundred. The battle was to last only nine hours.

On June 25, the Iraqis captured the oil-rich Majnoon Islands after only eight hours of fighting. Having pushed Iran from virtually all significant Iranian footholds in southern Iraq, the better-equipped, better-trained, and now more highly motivated Iraqi armed forces--spearheaded by the 100,000-man elite Republican Guard--had no problems in reconquering Iraq's northern Kurdish area, forcing back the last major concentration of Iranian troops.

HALABJA

The Fao offensive over, Saddam Hussein now turned his attention to the Iraqi Kurds. After the Iranians achieved a successful Iranian armored thrust against Iraqi positions in the northern sector of the front, the Iraqis counterattacked and threw the Iranians back. But this was not enough. The Iraqi air force and artillery launched an attack against the Kurdish town of Halabja, an attack that claimed more than 5,000 innocent civilians. For the most part the victims were young children and the elderly, completely unaware that Baghdad's air force would drop poison gas on the town and remorselessly flout the convention outlawing chemical warfare, an international treaty to which Iraq itself was a party. This episode was given scant attention in the Western media; it was treated as little better than a human-interest story at a time when the West was too preoccupied with Israel's almost daily suppression of the Palestinian *Intifada* uprising in its occupied territories. Arab newspapers ignored the event altogether; most printed anti-Kurdish articles, accusing the Kurds of working for Israel. The Kuwaiti press was the most vocal in its condemnation of the Kurds and in its support of Baghdad's crusade against them.

The poison gas attack turned out to be the single most enormous massacre of civilians in one place at one time since the Nazi atrocities. Yet Western commentators, especially before 1990, when it least concerned the West, very often liked to present Iraq's more moderate image in contrast with the more deviant and treacherous Iran. There were, however, some dissenting voices in the United States. The most vocal of the criticisms came from the *New Republic*'s editor-in-chief, Martin Peretz. To be sure, he was one of the few exceptions to the stone-like silence. The style of the accusation was fulminating and sweeping. Writing in his magazine's "Cambridge Diarist" column, he explicitly stated:

> The Kurds, a more ancient people with deeper attributes of nationhood than the most perfervid Palestinian tribunes could

possibly claim for themselves . . . it is a measure of the prevailing norms in Sunni Islam that these outrages have produced scarcely a shudder of discomfort from Iraq's allies, including most notably Saudi Arabia, Jordan, Egypt and the residual legatee of pan-Arabism, the PLO.[33]

In the same breath, Peretz reminded us how much perhaps Iraqi Shi'ites, the Kurds, and some Iranians owed to the former Israeli prime minister, the late Menachem Begin, for having destroyed Iraq's (Saddam Hussein's) nuclear reactor in 1981.[34]

Another exception came from American embassy staffers in Ankara. They interviewed and photographed Kurdish refugees. The CIA gave the U.S. State Department a confidential report pointing to Iraq's use of chemical weapons that included nerve agents and mustard gas against the Kurds. Televisions across the world showed the extent of the devastation, of murdered parents clutching babies on their doorsteps and in the streets of Halabja. The Red Cross reported that more than 100,000 Kurds had fled to Turkey. Most of the youngsters were severely burned by hydrogen cyanide. Secretary of State George Shultz finally said that the United States had evidence that Iraq had used chemical weapons against Kurdish villages. In September, the U.S. Senate Foreign Relations Committee sent two of its members on a fact-finding mission to Turkey.

The Foreign Relations Committee chairman, Claiborne Pell, tabled the Prevention of Genocide Act in the U.S. Senate, where he declared:

> While people are gassed, the world is largely silent. There are reasons for this: Iraq's great oil wealth, its military strength, a desire not to upset the delicate negotiations seeking an end to the Iran-Iraq War. Silence, however, is complicity. Half a century ago, the world was silent as Hitler began a campaign that culminated in the near extermination of Europe's Jews. We cannot be silent to genocide again.[35]

The Iraqis found it unreasonable to ask for a ban on chemical weapons when Israel possessed nuclear weapons. The Iraqi regime was not alone in its defense, which mainly amounted to denying the use of chemical weapons, with many wellwishers in the U.S. academic, military, and business establishment. Stephen C. Pelletiere, Douglas V. Johnson II, and Leif R. Rosenberger wrote a propaganda monograph two years later titled *Iraqi Power and U.S. Security in the Middle East* (Carlisle Barracks, Penn.: Strategic Studies Institute, U.S. Army War College, 1990), which questioned whether Iraq had ever used chemicals against the Kurdish population. The piece criticized George Shultz and the U.S. Senate for seeking to impose sanctions on Iraq after the gas attacks. The authors even asserted that it was the Iranians' gas that killed the Kurds at Halabja.[36]

The White House argued that sanctions would be counterproductive. The American presidential elections were just around the corner; Western and Iraqi business interests were budding. So the approval of a bill of sanctions by the U.S. House of Representatives against Iraq, to all intents and purposes, became irrelevant. The whole affair was then dropped.

DENOUEMENT

"I'll drink this bitter cup of poison," Khomeini remarked when he acquiesced in the ceasefire agreement, accepting U.N. Resolution 598. Iranian forces had been heavily battered on land, on the sea, and in the air. In July 1988, a further misfortune befell the Iranian nation. An Iran Air passenger plane had been mistakenly shot down by a U.S. man-of-war, the *Vincennes*, with the loss of 290 innocent persons on board. Khomeini himself was seriously ill, and Hashemi Rafsanjani thought that it was best to cease all hostilities for good. According to U.S. intelligence sources, on the evening of July 16 there was a meeting in Teheran of senior political officials, including Montazeri, Rafsanjani, Prime Minister Mir Hussein Moussavi, and Ahmed Khomeini, the Ayatollah's oldest son. Montazeri supported Rafsanjani, recommending that, in the interests of the revolution, the elder Khomeini should fall in line with the ceasefire. Khomeini's announcement was welcomed in every Arab capital in the Middle East. Only Israel felt misgivings about the end to the fighting between its two implacable foes.

In Teheran there was neither the time nor the desire now to discuss or think about the inherent failures of the Iranian military command, the "ifs," the "might-have-beens" in this long and grueling eight-year episode. The Iranians realized they could not detach themselves completely from either of the two superpowers. There was certainly only lackluster support for Khomeini's war effort among the Iranian public. Overtures to the United States for a better working relationship between Teheran and Washington were next on the political agenda.

But history will still have to explain other nagging questions. Why, for instance, did Iran not try to open another front against Iraq by attacking that country from across the Syrian border, to which Iraq had sent only 100,000 troops, a number insufficient to hold down a massive attack over very extensive lines of communication? The Iraqis would have been over-whelmed and forced to shift fresh troops from the south to that new and far weaker front. A more rational player in such a game of power politics and regional alliances, when the stakes are stacked against it, would not have eschewed military cooperation with a state like Israel, whose enemies have traditionally been the same as Iran's. In vain the Israelis made several overtures to the Iranians to assist in the struggle against Iraq.

The Israelis had always attempted to form something of a tacit Israel-Iran-Saudi Arabia alliance, trying to involve the less credulous Americans in this scheme. Back in October 1982 then Israeli ambassador to the United States Moshe Arens, long before the "Irangate" scandal burst forth on the world, informed the press that Israel was providing arms to Iran "in coordination with the U.S. government"--in the hope of establishing relations with Iranian officers who would carry out a military coup or who might be in a position of power in Iran during the post-Khomeini succession.[37] In this way, the Israelis, ever concerned about the outcome of the Iran-Iraq war, helped keep channels open to the moderate or pragmatic elements in Iran among both the clerics and the military--elements who might one day overthrow or inherit the power of the Shi'a leadership.

The end of the war in the Gulf started a debate in Israel as to what threat the Iraqi military now posed to Israel and to the entire Middle East. Some voices were even speaking about a more positive attitude toward Iraq, perceiving Saddam Hussein almost in the Mubarak (Egyptian) camp. But these were all in the minority; most politicians and political analysts in Israel felt that Iraq was more likely to return to its leadership of the anti-Israeli Arab coalition. A former U.S. National Security Council consultant, Michael Ledeen, broached the idea of a Washington-Teheran rapprochement from which Israel could benefit.[38] American magazine columnist Charles Krauthammer, biased against the Arabs in the extreme, also called for a "decisive [U.S.] geopolitical tilt toward Iran."[39] He was supported in Israel by the Mossad and by the top men in the Israeli military.[40] Brig. General Aharon Levran, head of the Middle East Balance project at Tel Aviv University's Jaffee Center of Strategic Studies, admitted that Iraq was a "major player" but did not think that the hostilities between these two Gulf powers had ended definitively.[41] Most disturbing to Israeli strategists at this point were Iraqi missile capabilities. Israeli Reserve Army Maj. General Sholom Gazit, former head of military intelligence, said that "one can say with certainty that the Iraqi Army will reach our border and will fight in a much more comprehensive way than we've known in the past."[42]

The Iraqis had certainly performed an admirable job of mobilizing the students in the country to reconstitute the Republican Guard. They performed splendidly by training the Guard and the rest of the army in offensive tactics and operations--in the latter battles, Iraq successfully paired the Guard with a regular army unit to gain specific objectives. Even when the Iraqis did not use chemical weapons or did not need to use them, the Iraqi army performed very well and prepared itself skillfully for each engagement.

The war with Iran taught the Iraqis valuable lessons. They learned how to fight both offensively and defensively, and their officers became better trained to lead battles. They learned how to effectively set up defensive lines, how to dig in with their weapons to create the maximum effect needed to destroy their enemies. The command structure grew less centralized, and operational skills vastly improved. Logistics improved considerably as well. They learned to use their new weapons more constructively and introduced the use of chemical weapons in a very useful, though brutal, way. Only the Iraqi air force was the weak link in the war. The only other weakness lay at the top. Whenever Saddam Hussein intervened in the decision-making process, it had a disastrous effect: it overrode conventional military wisdom. It was difficult for Saddam to allow his generals too much leeway.

All in all, Iraq had gained a number of advantages in the immediate aftermath of the war. Baghdad was able to normalize its relations with the United States and the USSR and entered into a strong economic and military supply relationship with France, Jordan (whose economy reached an unprecedented boom during this war), and Egypt. It could count on support and funds from Saudi Arabia, Kuwait, and the other Gulf Arabs. Finally, it received access to many sophisticated and complete weapons systems from the major powers.[43] Iraq and Saddam Hussein had gained important friends and wellwishers abroad. Saddam exercised a spell not only on the Third World, but on the majority of Arabs in the Middle East. Saddam's endurance, his hazardous and complicated military undertakings requiring prodigies of careful organization, endeared him and his regime to American military analysts, academics, and think-tank consultants (we shall come back to this issue as the narrative unfolds). Europeans themselves, such as the French defense minister, Jean-Pierre Chevènement, heaped praise upon praise for Saddam Hussein's moderation, setting the tone for French business to get more involved in the Iraqi defense sector. Chevènement unabashedly founded an Iraqi-French friendship society, and there was still much more to come from the rest of Europe and the United States. Read on!

This long and bloody war ended with a serious miscalculation on the part of Saddam Hussein: he believed he was invincible and disregarded the major lessons of history. *Qadissiyat Saddam* may have cost as many as 1.7 million lives, including civilian casualties. *Jane's Defence Weekly* estimated the total number killed by September 1986 at one million.[44] A Soviet correspondent of *Literaturnaia Gazetta*, K. Kapitonov, offered an estimate of 600-700,000 Iranian casualties and 400-500,000 Iraqi casualties.[45] Non-combat deaths included the loss of 37 Americans at sea on board the USS *Stark* as a result of an Iraqi attack in 1987 and approximately 475 merchant shipping seamen who died in attacks during the tanker war.[46] The cost of rebuilding and reequipping industry was estimated to run into the hundreds of millions of dollars. Kiyotaki Tsuji of the Japanese Institute of Middle Eastern Studies estimates lost oil revenues at \$23 billion for Iran and \$65 billion for Iraq.[47] Iraq owed tens of billions to Kuwaiti, Saudi Arabian, European, Japanese, and Soviet bloc creditors while Iran owed approximately \$5 billion in short-term loans from foreign banks.[48]

Nor did this mean that Iran had been defeated militarily after Iranian troops pulled out of Iraqi territory in July 1988. Iran's politicians were simply not willing to give up at the bargaining table what the military leaders did not concede on the battlefield. Iran still insisted on the full implementation of the 1975 agreements. A stalemate was to last for two more years. But in two years the world was in for another surprise. "The Iraqi nation is invincible," Saddam naively proclaimed. All it meant was that one war had ended, another one was to begin; this time Iran would be sitting on the sidelines, watching.

NOTES

1.   Aaron Davis, "Iraqi Army: Operations and Doctrine," *Military Intelligence*, April-June 1991, p. 9. See also Miron Rezun, ed., *Iran at the Crossroads: Global Relations in a Turbulent Decade* (Boulder: Westview, 1990), and Shahram Chubin and Charles Tripp, *Iran and Iraq at War* (Boulder: Westview, 1988).

2.   *Washington Post*, August 19, 1987.

3.   With the exception of the covert actions of the United States in an infamous incident dubbed the "Iran-Contra Scandal." In order to gain the release of hostages being held by the Iranian-backed Hezbollah party in Lebanon, the White House authorized the sale of weapons, via Israel, to Iran. The money from the sale was then diverted to the Nicaraguan Contras, who were fighting the pro-Soviet Sandinista government.

4.   Abel Darwish and Gregory Alexander, *Unholy Babylon* (London: Victor Gollancz Ltd., 1991), p. 61.

5.   *The Economist*, January 30, 1988.

6.   Ibid., p. 34.

7.   *Keyhan*, March 7, 1986.

8.   Jeffrey Record, "The OS Central Command: Toward What Purpose?," *Strategic Review*, Spring 1986, p. 44.

9.   Shahram Chubin, "Iran and the War," in Rezun, *Iran at the Crossroads*, p. 137.

10.   International Institute of Strategic Studies (IISS), *Military Balance, 1984-1988*.

11.   See *Baghdad Home Service*, November 14, 1988 on the BBC; and also see *Summary of World Broadcasts*, ME/0311/A/9, November 17, 1988.

12.   Ibid.

13. *The Economist*, June 4, 1988, p. 14.

14. Darwish and Alexander, *Unholy Babylon*, p. 65. The account is taken from pp. 64 and 65.

15. See Miron Rezun, *Intrigue and War in Southwest Asia* (New York: Praeger, 1991).

16. Stephen C. Pelletiere, *The Kurds: An Unstable Element in the Gulf* (Boulder: Westview, 1984), p. 184.

17. Ibid., p. 187.

18. Ibid.

19. Ibid. See chapter on Saddam Hussein in Rezun, *Intrigue and War in Southwest Asia*.

20. "Opposition Regroups," in *Afkar-Inquiry*, February 1987, p. 9.

21. Ibid., p. 8.

22. Iqbal Asaria, p. 7.

23. Ibid.

24. *Christian Science Monitor*, July 8, 1988.

25. Howard Chua-Eoan, "Arrows in Our Chests," *Time*, January 11, 1988.

26. The GCC broke with Egypt when Cairo and Tel Aviv made peace in 1979. Only Oman maintained its links with Egypt.

27. In a study likely to endure as the best of its kind on this subject, there are many direct and subtle references to this U.S. interference; nor is any evidence lacking in support of the argument that the Iraqis began using poison gas against the Iranian offensives as early as 1984 and then again in 1985 and 1986. See Chubin and Tripp, *Iran and Iraq at War*.

28. *Time*, January 11, 1988.

29. Edgar O'Ballance, *The Gulf War* (London: Brassey's, 1988), p. 70.

30. Anthony Cordesman and Abraham R. Wagner. *The Lessons of Modern War, volume 2: The Iran-Iraq War* (Boulder: Westview, 1990), pp. 354-355.

31. Captain Michael E. Bigelow, "The Faw Peninsula: A Battle Analysis," *Military Intelligence*, April-June 1991, vol. 17, no. 2, p. 16.

32. Ibid., p. 17.

33. Martin Peretz, "Cambridge Diarist," *The New Republic*, May 1988.

34. Ibid. On June 8, 1981, Israel took advantage of Iraq's preoccupation with the war to bomb and destroy the Iraqi nuclear reactor in Tammuz, where Saddam Hussein was undertaking experiments to develop an atom bomb. For a dramatic account of the Israeli air strike against the nuclear reactor, called Osirak, see Dan McKinnon, *Bullseye Iraq* (New York: Berkley Books, 1987).

35. Quoted in Darwish and Alexander, *Unholy Babylon*, p. 81.

36. For a debate of this subject between the writers above and

Edward Mortimer, a British journalist for the *Financial Times* and author of *Faith and Power* (one of the best books written on Islam and politics), see the *New York Review of Books*, November 22, 1990.

37. For an interesting discussion of clandestine Israeli and U.S. activities in Iran, see Noam Chomsky, *The Culture of Terrorism* (Montreal, New York: Black Rose Books, 1988), chapter 8.

38. *New York Times*, July 19, 1988, I, p. 31. Michael Ledeen played a key role in linking the White House with Israeli officials to win influence in Iran.

39. *Washington Post*, September 16, 1988.

40. See Leviticus, "Iraq: Soon a Major Player," in *Israel and Palestine Political Report*, no. 143, August 1988, p. 6.

41. *Christian Science Monitor*, July 20, 1988.

42. *New York Times*, July 24, 1988.

43. Chubin and Tripp, *Iran and Iraq at War*, p. 2.

44. *Jane's Defence Weekly*, vol. 6, no. 11, September 20, 1988, p. 759.

45. K. Kapitonov, *Literaturnaia Gazetta*, May 11, 1988.

46. *Christian Science Monitor*, August 12, 1988, as quoted by John Sigler in "The Legacy of the Iran-Iraq War," in Rezun, *Iran at the Cross-roads*.

47. *Washington Post*, August 18, 1988, as quoted by John Sigler, ibid.

48. Ibid.

4

The Signals Were There—
but No One Listened

Iraq was not invincible, not by any stretch of the imagination. Under Saddam's leadership, the country had played its cards right; it neither alienated the Soviet Union nor the United States. Baghdad played one superpower off against the other, without really being a client of either. For war material it depended on both. It was heavily indebted to Western Europe, too. But Iraq was doing a lot better than Syria. Moscow had all but given up its stake in al-Assad's Ba'athist regime. So Syria was no longer the privileged Arab client state. Iraq needed the support of a mighty superpower. But the Soviet Union was passing through a period of social turbulence, economic disorder, and political anarchy. Moscow was loath to antagonize the West. Moscow needed Western credits and investments in its agonizing transition to a market economy. The Soviets were the last nation on earth one could count on for material assistance.

Saddam knew he could not fight a prolonged war against a superpower like the United States in the Gulf. Alone he could not fight and win against Israel any more than Syria could. There were approximately 500 miles separating Iraq from the Israeli frontier, and Israel could only be reached by Soviet-built Scud missiles or by a Jordanian proxy fighting force. In any event, Saddam had been getting signals that the U.S. government was bent on improving relations with Iraq at any price. He imagined that the Americans could get their media to become more pliant, in the way it usually happened with the Arab states. He saw himself leading a crusade, a just cause on behalf of all the Arabs, starting with the Kuwaitis and the Palestinians. He imagined he also had all of Islam on his side.

Saddam lulled himself into thinking he was invincible. A man flushed with victory can easily come to believe his own imaginings, that he can cripple any determined foe who stands in his way. It was perhaps Saddam's way of exaggerating things, in keeping with the old Arab way of over-assertion.

Slyer than a fox, Saddam proved to be maliciously practical in preparing his next move: the occupation of Kuwait and the domination of the Gulf's oil sheikhdoms, possibly appropriating their wealth, their lands, their oil, their manpower, and their resources. He did not think this was irrational, not any more brazen than invading Iran. Kuwait, which had served as an extended shoreline and second port for Iraq during the long siege of Basra, had always been coveted by the Iraqis. Kuwait would not resist, indeed, could not resist. The other Gulf states might resist but would fall like dominoes once they had witnessed how easy it was for Iraq to conquer Kuwait.

And what of the Americans? They could be won over diplomatically. What of the other Arab states? They could be bought off or bullied or subverted. What about Iran? There was as yet no peace treaty with that country. Maybe Iran could be co-opted into working with Saddam to share the wealth of the whole Gulf region.

Carefully scheming every move, weighing each opportunity, Saddam made it no secret that he was angered at the insistence of the Kuwaitis that he pay them back what he owed them. Kuwait's emir, Jabir al-Ahmad al-Sabah, was keeping the world prices of oil very low and crippling Iraq when the latter was struggling to pay over $100 billion in war debts. The Ba'athists had always had a genuine disgust for those Arab reactionary forces: the wealthy oil sheiks, propped up by the U.S. Government and the CIA, were hated by the vast majority of the Arab poor.

The Iraqi president was able to reach the disenfranchised Arab masses through newspapers. One could finance the Arab media and better shape the collective mind of the Arabs by sheer bribery. Saddam's Ministry of Information paid out $2 million to suborn Arab diplomats, analysts, rivals, and anyone else who could run a pro-Saddam Arab press that criticized all Arabs who had not assisted Iraq in the war. The press attacked Zionism and Western imperialism. Some of these articles even hinted, with the help of maps and diagrams, that if Iraq had had access to the Kuwaiti island of Bubiyan and if it had a longer shoreline than its mere 37 kilometers, it would have defeated Iran earlier in the war.

Whenever Arab newspaper editors arrived in Baghdad for handouts, they complained bitterly about the lack of funds while the Arab oil magnates squandered exorbitant sums in European casinos. Saddam received the London-based or New York-based or Paris-based editors with open arms, giving the Saudis and Kuwaitis a dressing-down: "Their [the sheikhs'] help is not enough and not coming from the heart; they don't give a damn about the Arab nation. They just want us to stop Khomeini getting to them. But wait until we finish this war; then Arab soldiers will get their rightful share of Arab wealth." These were subtle, veiled threats against the opulence of the Gulf sheikhs. The pro-Saddam press put hundreds of Arab journalists on Baghdad's payroll. The messages against the "mean sheikhs" rang clear across the European capitals where the Arab diplomats and businessmen hobnobbed and wealthy Arab tourists doubled as play-boys in search of adventure and property. "They are spending the wealth of the Arab nation," Saddam remarked, "in the United States and in Europe, which support the Zionist butchers." In one diatribe, the Arab press in England reminded its readers that only 20 percent of the people in Kuwait were allowed to vote; incidentally, women had no vote at all.

Much of the oil wealth in Iraq was allowed to filter down through the population. In contrast to other Gulf regimes, there seemed to be a positive effort by Baghdad to emancipate and educate its women. Spending in Iraq was at an all-time high. Instead of curbing it, the Iraqi treasury was given the go-ahead by Saddam to increase it. And all the while there was the feeling in Iraq that the Gulf Arabs, even the United States, were not suffi-ciently grateful for Iraq's sacrifice in the war.

Iraq had been excluded from the GCC from the very beginning. Saddam did not think this fair. He did not have any love for the Arab League either. So Saddam began pressing the idea of creating an Arab Co-operation Council (ACC), to include Egypt, Iraq, North Yemen, and Jordan. The agreement was signed a few months before Khomeini's death on the nineteenth of February 1989, and it was to serve as a kind of binding Arab Common Market. The signs were clearly positive; the West immediately interpreted it as an economic union--which it was not--and falsely reasoned that since Saddam was drawing closer to such pragmatic leaders as President Mubarak of Egypt and King Hussein of Jordan then it was all for the good, the implication being that Iraq's radical course in foreign policy had come to an end. The West also was failing to realize that King Hussein was supporting Saddam's general policy of getting the rich Arab countries to foot the bill for the poorer ones.

What the West did not suspect was Saddam's behind-the-scenes maneuvering. For one thing, he was adopting a more anti-Western tone, especially during the period of the Bazoft affair (more on this later). It was frustrating for Saddam to have to experience problems in attracting foreign entrepreneurs to invest in Iraq's state-owned businesses, while Western Europe and the United States were willing to sell weapons and offered fantastic lines of credit. On a visit to see Hosni Mubarak in Egypt in the early part of 1990, he took the Egyptian leader aside and proposed a military coalition of Iraq, Egypt, Syria, and Jordan. They would pool their resources and carve up Kuwait and Saudi Arabia. Egypt, Saddam prom-ised, would get $25 billion in spoils.

The following month, Saddam offered Yemen (then North Yemen) two of Saudi Arabia's oil-rich southern provinces, O'ssiran and Najran,

which Ibn Saud had annexed in 1934 with the blessing of the British. On
another occasion, he told Jordan's king that he may as well have the
western part of the Saudi peninsula. Characteristically, Saddam then went
and called upon Saudi Arabia's King Fahd to tell him that all the coastal
Gulf states "didn't make any sense" and literally told the Saudi monarch
that he was going to annex Kuwait. He added that the Saudis should "take
Qatar."

None of these signals were being taken seriously. Saddam had barely
terminated a war with Iran that could erupt again at any minute. The
Kuwaitis in particular were having problems with the Palestinian segment
of their population, and there was a strong Shi'a movement that was
pacified with great difficulty. Iraq was still perceived as a protector by the
al-Sabah ruling family. But in the past Iraq did make innumerable claims
on Kuwait. The emirate had been a part of the Basra "vilayet" province of
Iraq during Ottoman times. Only in 1897 did Kuwait become a British pro-
tectorate, which prevented Iraq from overtly attacking a country enjoying
the support of a strong British military force. In the inter-war period the
legitimacy of Kuwait's sovereignty was frequently called into question.

In 1937, King Ghazi of Iraq called for Kuwait to be annexed as part
of Iraq following a period of poor economic growth in Kuwait. Ghazi tried
to foment dissent in Kuwait and moved his troops to the border. Only a
British threat to intervene and the death of King Ghazi in a car accident in
1939 prevented the invasion. In 1961, when the British gave Kuwait full
independence, Iraq's leader, Abdul Karim Qassim, claimed Kuwait for Iraq.
Still in exile, Saddam Hussein quickly sent a telegram to Qassim approving
of his attempts to annex Kuwait. Iraqi newspapers rang out: "Kuwait is part
of Iraq, we are one nation, separated by the criminal knife of British
imperialism."[1]

The British embassy in Iraq went out of its way to provide the government with information and warned the Iraqis that Britain would react
aggressively to any Iraqi invasion. Qassim's tactics, later imitated by
Hussein in 1990, included the dispatch of a massive army deployment to
the Kuwaiti border under cover of troop rehearsals for the Iraqi National
Day parade; the sending of Iraqi intelligence agents to Kuwait in order to
instigate riots; and planting false stories concerning atrocities against Iraqis
by Britons, Zionists, and the CIA spies as an excuse to dispatch troops to
Kuwait. To sidestep the threat, Kuwait was allowed into the Arab League
and League forces entered Kuwait in September of 1961, thus discour-
aging an Iraqi attack. Iraq subsequently withdrew from the Arab League
because of this.

In 1973, the Ba'ath government occupied a border post in Kuwait in
order to gain access to two Kuwaiti islands, Bubiyan and Warbah, and they
did not withdraw their troops until 1977. In 1978, Saddam proposed a
union with Syria in which Kuwait and Saudi Arabia would be taken over

unless the other Arab countries agreed to punish Egypt for its peace treaty with Israel by breaking off all diplomatic and economic ties. Needless to say, the Arab countries quickly broke their ties with Egypt.

Other points that transpired from conversations with the Iraqis were only belatedly reported. Iraq had spoken out against Kuwait's overproduction of oil: an overproduction that drove down the price of oil and cost Iraq substantial foreign exchange earnings (Iraq depends upon oil for 95 percent of its foreign exchange earnings). Hussein not only believed that this was in direct violation of OPEC quotas but represented a danger to all Mideastern economies, his own especially. Hussein was also involved in a quarrel with Kuwait over the Rumaila oil fields, which straddle both countries. During the Iran-Iraq war, Hussein had accused Kuwait of moving the border between the two countries northward so that Kuwait could pump oil from the Iraqi field, through a method known as slant drilling. He sought approximately $2.4 billion in compensation.

Coveting Bubiyan and Warbah islands off the coast of Kuwait was patently logical. Since Iraq possesses no more than 37 kilometers of shoreline, these islands, in effect, dramatically cut off effective access to Iraq's main port at Umm Qasr. Warbah Island is itself a large sandbar, and Iraq was hoping to see it dredged out of existence. Bubiyan Island could therefore be turned into an effective port for Iraqi oil tankers. Iraq has long had the distinct disadvantage of having no seaport, and Saddam felt that in this way he could supply his country with just such a resource. The Iraqi port of Basra on the Shatt-al-Arab estuary (formed by the merging of the Tigris and Euphrates rivers) had become useless, since it was full of mines and wreckage left over from the Iran-Iraq war.

While most Arab states were ignoring Saddam Hussein, disregarding the signals he was giving about his intentions in the Gulf region, the Kuwaitis, who were concerned about Saddam's intentions, did not know what to make of him. At the beginning of 1990, the Kuwaitis made ready to send a high-powered delegation to Iraq to sign a non-aggression pact with the Iraqi president. Sheikh Sa'ad al-Abdallah al-Salem al-Sabah (also of the al-Sabah family), who was prime minister of Kuwait, went to Baghdad for a talk with Saddam Hussein. The latter told the Kuwaiti prime minister that he would like to lease the two Kuwaiti islands, Bubiyan and Warbah. Saddam said it was necessary for the security of Iraq's Gulf port of Umm Qasr. Saddam was riding his guest roughshod, and the meeting ended in a stalemate.

Saddam had few advisors, but those few he had he was eager to listen to. When they were not related to him or were not members of the Iraqi Revolutionary Command Council, they were important ministers in his government. One was Tariq Aziz, his foreign minister, a Christian and a staunch Ba'ath supporter; the other was Mohammed al-Mashat, Iraqi ambassador to the United States, an unscrupulous man who did not balk from feeding the Iraqi dictator information he knew to be untrue. Both these men were assuring Saddam that by combining the OPEC quotas of Iraq and Kuwait and by forcing prices up to $30 a barrel, Saddam would get at least $16 billion each year. In this way, Iraq could double its development budget and still pay off its debts within four years. They and others prompted Saddam to expand Iraq's coastline from a mere 37 kilometers to 225 kilometers and wind up with a deepwater port. They kept feeding Saddam's already magnified delusions.

Sitting in the Iraqi embassy off Duport Circle in Washington, the chain-smoking al-Mashat was warning Saddam about the Israeli and American media. "I've begun to suspect that there is some kind of conspiracy to destabilize Iraq," he complained in message after message. There had indeed been some criticism of companies around the world who were competing for Iraqi arms orders.

The world press relentlessly began to criticize the Baghdad regime for another reason. The Iranian-born journalist Farzad Bazoft[2] had been apprehended and executed by the Iraqi regime for having strayed far out beyond Baghdad's city limits investigating an explosion at a factory at Al-Hillah with a British nurse, Daphne Parish. The Iraqi *Mukhabarat* forced a confession out of him saying he was spying for Israel and Britain.

Gerald Bull, the Canadian arms manufacturer and inventor of "Project Babylon," had been assassinated a year previously by Israeli Mossad agents in Europe. Bull had been working on a powerful supergun, the world's most powerful artillery piece, which, with devastating accuracy, was seemingly capable of firing chemical and possibly even nuclear shells as far as Israel. On March 28, 1990, British customs and excise officers, with the help of the U.S. Customs Service, were able to apprehend a group of Iraqis and Britons who were attempting to smuggle krypton capacitators out of Britain for Iraq's nuclear program.

Israel at this point was becoming extremely skittish about Iraq's armed might. Israel's government had absolutely no link with Bazoft; the London-based journalist had been working for the *Observer*, and his visit to the Iraqi explosion site was a routine affair. Nor was he spying for Iran.

Yet Saddam Hussein seemed to be getting what he wanted from this story. He was successfully whipping up the Arab population against Israel and the British. His advisors were repeatedly telling him that if al-Assad was entitled to invade Lebanon, if Israel was entitled to keep the Occupied Territories, why then should Saddam be denied the equal right of occupying an illegitimate Arab state? They impressed on him that chemical weapons were a factor the Israelis took very seriously. Besides, if it did come to war with Israel, he would have the backing of the whole Arab world, the Egyptian masses, and the whole Palestinian people. The Israelis could not absorb even a thousand dead, given their population, and the war would stop the Jews from immigrating to Israel from the Soviet Union.

Israeli television and newspapers, in the meantime, debated the option of destroying Iraq's chemical capability, just like the Israelis did in June 1981 when they destroyed the Iraqi nuclear reactor. Israel's Arab-language programs were focusing on Saddam Hussein's "mad adventurism."

Taking a cue from the Israeli press, on February 15 the Voice of America condemned Hussein as one of the worst tyrants in the world. The radio program called "No More Secret Police" reminded its listeners that 1990 ought to be like 1989, when dictators were toppled, when nations became free. The moderator, an American Jew, started the program with the statement: "The success of dictatorial rule and tyranny requires the existence of a large secret police, while the success of democracy requires the abolishment of such a force." The announcer also compared Saddam Hussein to the deposed Romanian leader Nicolae Ceausescu.

These occurrences more or less prompted a series of signals that were misread, misconstrued, glossed over, ignored, forgiven, and forgotten by the Americans and the British. The first was Hussein's broadcast over Jordanian television on February 24 during a meeting of the ACC in Jordan. In this speech, Hussein spoke out against the United States and its policies in the Gulf. He stated that eventually the United States would take over the Gulf in order to satisfy its own need for oil. He called for the Americans "to get out of the Gulf." On February 19, Saddam stated; "I need $30 billion in fresh money. Go and tell them in Saudi Arabia and the Gulf that if they don't give it to me, I will know how to take it."[3] This should have given the West pause. It clearly pointed out his regional plans. But most analysts believed that this was merely more of Saddam's telltale bellicosity. Washington did not believe that Saddam was changing his policies. The Americans simply felt it was an overreaction by an angry Arab leader to a recent broadcast by the Voice of America.

In fact, U.S. Undersecretary John Kelly complained to Secretary of State James Baker, who in turn ordered the U.S. Information Service not to produce any editorial without prior clearance from the State Department. On April 12, five U.S. senators visited Iraq. The five senators--Robert Dole, Alan Simpson, Howard Metzenbaum, James McClure, and Frank Murkowski--including U.S. Ambassador to Baghdad April Glaspie, attended a meeting with Saddam Hussein in Mosul, in Iraqi Kurdistan. The meeting came at a time when Hussein had threatened Israel with chemical weapons if it were ever to attack Iraq. "By God," he complained, "we will make the fire eat up half of Israel, if it tries to do anything against Iraq."[4] Congress's object in sending these representatives was to consider imposing trade sanctions against Iraq. President George Bush certainly knew about their mission. But what was that mission all about? The record eloquently shows how the senators all cringed and lied and completely misunderstood Saddam's motives.

The following is a transcript of the exchange between the Iraqi president and the senators. The reader will first note how useless it was to send the American Jewish senator, Metzenbaum, to meet with Saddam. It was also a barefaced lie to tell Saddam that the man responsible for the Voice of America broadcast had been sacked or even to intimate that he would be sacked. The reader will also note their pusillanimity when confronted with the Iraqi dictator, a fact that was celebrated by the pro-Saddam Arab press.

President Saddam Hussein: Daily the Arabs hear scorn directed at them from the West, daily they bear insults. Why? Has the Zionist mentality taken control of you to the point that it has deprived you of your humanity? . . .

Senator Dole: There are fundamental differences between our countries. We have free media in the U.S. When you say "Western," Mr. President--I don't know what you mean when you say "the West." I don't know whether or not you mean the government. There is a person who did not have the authority to say anything about . . . [your] government. He was a commentator for the VOA (the Voice of America, which represents the government only) and this person was removed from it. Please allow me to say that only 12 hours earlier President Bush had assured me that he wants better relations, and that the U.S. government wants better relations with Iraq. We believe--and we are leaders in the U.S. Congress--that the Congress also does not represent Bush or the government. I assume that President Bush will oppose sanctions, and he might veto them, unless something provocative were to happen, or something of that sort.

. . .

Senator Dole: We in the Congress are also striving to do what we can in this direction. The president may differ with the Congress, and if there is a divergent viewpoint, he has the right to express it, and to exercise his authority concerning it.

. . .

Senator Simpson: I enjoy meeting candid and open people. This is a trademark of those of us who live in the "Wild West." ... One of the reasons that we telephoned President Bush yesterday evening was to tell the President that our visit to Iraq would cost us a great deal of popularity, and that many people would attack us for coming to Iraq. . . . But President Bush said, "Go there. I want you there. . . . If you are criticized because of your visit to Iraq, I will defend you and speak on your behalf." . . . Democracy is a very confusing issue. I believe that your problems lie with the Western media and not with the U.S. government. As long as you are isolated from the media, the press--and it is a haughty and pampered press; they all consider themselves politi- cal geniuses, that is, the journalists do; they are very cynical-- what I advise is that you invite them to come here and see for themselves.

Hussein: They are welcome. We hope that they will come to see Iraq and, after they do, write whatever they like . . . [But] I wonder, as you may wonder, if governments, for example, the U.S. government, were not behind such reports [negative news stories about Iraq]. How else could all of this [negative media coverage of Iraq] have occurred in such a short period of time?

Simpson: It's very easy. . . . They all live off one another. Every- one takes from the other. When there is a major news item on the front page of the *New York Times*, another journalist takes it and publishes it.

. . .

Senator Metzenbaum: Mr. President, perhaps you have been given some information on me beforehand. I am a Jew and a staunch supporter of Israel. I did have some reservations on whether I should come on this visit.

Hussein: You certainly will not regret it afterward.

Metzenbaum: I do not regret it. Mr. President, you view the Western media in a very negative light. I am not the right person to be your public-relations man, but allow me to suggest a few things, as I am more concerned about peace than I am about any other particular factor. I do not want to talk about whether the entire West Bank should be given up, or half of Jerusalem, or any other parts [of Israel]. This issue should be left to the parties concerned. However, I have been sitting here and listen- ing to you for about an hour, and I am now aware that you are a strong and intelligent man and that you want peace. But I am also convinced that if you were to focus on the value of the peace that we greatly need to achieve in the Middle East then there would not be a leader to compare with you in the Middle East. I believe, Mr. President, that you can be a very influential force for peace in the Middle East. But, as I said, I am not your public-relations man.[5]

The foregoing conversation in itself may not have been a sign of the approach of war. It only illustrated to what extent Saddam Hussein was being pampered and lionized, which made him feel superior to Western leaders. The episode smacked of Hitler's encounter with the Western leaders--Chamberlain and Deladier--at Munich, when the German Führer watched them cowering, avoiding the inevitable. Here was a sure sign that Saddam had reached the zenith of his power, a power that was felt throughout the Middle East. Western leaders ought not to have pleaded and appealed to his reason. In the Middle East one must never appeal to reason; that is a sign of weakness--one must first exhibit force and then begin to talk about reason, within reason.

A third signal followed on May 28 when, at an Arab League summit meeting in Baghdad, Hussein denounced the Arab states for keeping oil prices too low and thereby declaring an "economic war" against Iraq. Again the Americans and British ignored these statements.

By mid-July of 1990 there was a special meeting of the Arab League's foreign ministers, who gathered to discuss the effects of the immigration of Soviet Jews to Israel. Iraq's tough and arrogant Tariq Aziz addressed a long and tedious note to the secretary-general of the Arab League, Chadli Kleibi, suggesting that Iraq's debts to its fellow Arabs should be written off, with an open accusation against Kuwait and the United States specifically.

He said:

Kuwait, with the complicity of the United Arab Emirates, has hatched a plot to inundate the oil market with a surplus far in excess of the quota allocated by OPEC. . . . Having explained the situation to all our brothers before, during, and after the Baghdad summit, having directly asked the two governments involved to put an end to this destructive policy because of the enormous damage it was causing, having sent envoys and letters, we condemn the action of the governments of Kuwait and the Emirates, considering it a direct act of aggression against Iraq and, clearly, against the whole Arab nation. . . . All sincere Arabs agree that the war Iraq had to wage was not merely in defense of her own sovereignty but also in defense of the eastern flank of the Arab world and of the whole Arab nation, especially the Gulf region. The Gulf leaders themselves admitted it openly.[6]

The fourth signal came on July 17th during Hussein's "Revolution Day Speech" when he launched into a verbal attack against Kuwait and the United Arab Emirates over their oil policies, calling them "puppets of the imperialist-Zionist interests which want to conquer the Arab world." The London-based *Economist* commented that the diatribe sounded "alarmingly like a pretext for invasion."[7] Again, the West ignored the warning.

The final signal occurred on July 24 when two Iraqi armored divisions were moved into position on the Kuwaiti border.

On the 25th, the American ambassador to Iraq, Canadian-born April Glaspie, was summoned to a meeting with Hussein. During the interview, Saddam pointed out that he knew what the United States was all about. Baghdad had been receiving false signals from the not-too-committed Ba'athist Mohammed al-Mashat, who was not above stroking Saddam's ego. Saddam's man in Washington was probably telling him that the United States had not sent troops when Turkey invaded Cyprus, it did not interfere when China invaded Tibet, nor did it intrude in force when the Soviet Union invaded Afghanistan. So there was no reason to worry; Saddam could stand tough with Bush's ambassador.

When the meeting with Ambassador Glaspie finally got under way, Saddam was polite but extremely condescending. After making a rambling exaggeration about how mighty Iraq was being threatened by tiny Kuwait, he intimated to her that "yours is a society which cannot accept 10,000 dead in one battle." His speech was peppered with exaggerated statements and overemphatic assertions. Then he stressed, even overstressed how "Iran agreed to the ceasefire not because the United States had bombed one of the oil platforms after the liberation of the Fao. Is this Iraq's reward for its role in securing the stability of the region and for protecting it from an unknown flood?"[8]

When Hussein's tone carried overt threats, Glaspie should have responded in kind, adding more emphasis to whatever she said. She should have been just as assertive. Too diplomatic, too cautious a person to engage in a rebuttal, she came across as being overly matter-of-fact. She might have stressed the possible implications an attack on Kuwait would have on Iraqi-American relations. Saddam chose to misread her, especially when she told him that the Americans would not take sides in a border dispute. Glaspie ought to have been categorical, perhaps more forcefully demanding, saying something like "No, no, definitely not, absolutely not, out of the question--I say no, my president would never allow you to threaten or invade a neighboring country. You must positively not even speak the way you're speaking." But a lowly foreign Ambassador could not possibly take a tone like that with the Iraqi ruler!

Nor would it be fair to blame Glaspie for sending mixed signals. That she was not doing her job properly was not her fault: diplomacy, in general, has its limitations. Open conflict is the only other way to conduct business. This interview was but one factor in a series of precipitating events that led to Hussein's decision to invade his tiny southern neighbor. If anyone was to blame, it must have been Glaspie's superior officers, who did not keep her abreast of the realities of the situation.

And what were those realities? The first was obvious: That in the month of July Saddam Hussein was massing huge forces on the Kuwaiti border. Washington had satellite photographs to prove it--there was a tremendous movement of Iraqi armor and infantry heading south. On the 29th of July, a CIA report showed that Iraqi forces numbered some 100,000 troops, supported by 300 battle tanks. Egypt's Mubarak was getting the same reports from his own intelligence services.

As early as May of that year, the CIA had already reported to the White House that Iraq was expected to attack Kuwait and the United Arab Emirates. An Israeli delegation of military and political experts also came to tell the White House of an impending attack on Kuwait. The White House and the Pentagon took this seriously, but pretended in the subsequent press releases that the information was treated with skepticism.[9] Some political analysts in Washington felt that Saddam was bluffing. It seems to me that these analysts were officially ignored.

On July 28, George Bush sent a message to Saddam Hussein which stressed that the use of force to resolve Iraq's problems with Kuwait was not acceptable and the United States would support its other friends in the Gulf. However, like the earlier message given by April Glaspie, it also stressed the desire to improve relations with Iraq.[10]

I am rather reluctant to seriously believe in conspiracy theories. It would be such a simple matter to suggest that the U.S. State Department was waiting for Saddam to make his move on Kuwait and had allowed Glaspie to feed him false information.

Conspiracies have indeed taken place, and there are precedents for this in the American past. I do believe that President John F. Kennedy may have been the victim of a conspiracy. Several people may have plotted Kennedy's murder, which was not the work of a single gunman. But how much of this actually implicated the U.S. government remains purely speculative--the stuff of movies.

Curiously, April Glaspie left for the United States on July 30th for an extended vacation. Should we read something into this? Was she not planted on Saddam Hussein by the State Department, and then taken away? What was the role of the White House in all this?

Again, this is purely speculative. In a crisis situation like this one, American military chiefs would certainly have their President's ear. The U.S. Congress must ratify any decision to go to war, but the President himself and the White House staff would enjoy primacy in decision-making. Even the American national security staff takes precedence over the State Department's career diplomats. As one perceptive journalist has observed:

"The President's national security staff can read the incoming electronic mail from around the globe and contact any embassy or CIA operation without ever informing State or CIA headquarters, as Oliver North often did. That means the White House can step into any issue at any time in any place."[11] Does this mean that the White House itself was communicating with April Glaspie? Even Schwarzkopf's memoirs will not clear this matter up.

Officials in Washington were playing a waiting game. Behind the scenes something must have been afoot--but, officially, all the war signals in the Gulf were astutely and conveniently ignored. No one listened, or pretended not to listen.

For many years, historians will, no doubt, debate the exact American political agenda. The questions one would now like to ask are: Why did U.S. policy-makers choose to ignore these warnings? Why did they choose to do nothing when it must have been obvious that Hussein had not changed from the man who had brazenly invaded Iran ten years before? How could they honestly believe that this man who had violently murdered his own people, a man who would stoop to any intrigue, would now suddenly hesitate to invade an Arab neighbor?

During the Iran-Iraq war itself, Americans found themselves in a position where they needed to choose sides. Having cut off relations with Iraq in the mid-1970s and having been subjected to the indignity of enduring a hostage crisis in Iran, they chose to follow the philosophy of "the enemy of my enemy is my friend" and selected the lesser of two evils--in this particular case, Iraq. The United States took Iraq off of its list of countries that sponsored terrorism after Hussein made the token gesture of expelling Palestinian terrorist Abu Nidal from Baghdad. This was obviously not a serious attempt by Iraq to show its non-support of terrorism. However, the United States seemed to be willing to accept this in order to use Iraq against Iran. Official relations were reestablished between Washington and Baghdad in 1984. Graham Fuller, who was a Mideast specialist with the CIA in the early 1980s, said:

> There was a genuine visceral fear of Islam in Washington as a force that was utterly alien to American thinking, and that really scared us. Senior people at the Pentagon and elsewhere were much more concerned about Islam than communism. It was an almost obsessive fear, leading to a mentality on our part that you should use any stick to beat a dog--to stop the advance of Islamic fundamentalism.[12]

Iraq thus became that stick.

These are clearly double standards. It is plain to see that American administrations have been more considerate to those who do not threaten

American interests. For example, the Americans balked from pressing a U.N. condemnation of Iraq for invading Iran insofar as that policy would have helped Iran, a nation so clearly anti-American--judging from the way American embassy workers were taken hostage in Teheran only ten years before. Kuwait, on the other hand, was a U.S. ally that provided Americans with vast amounts of oil; and to be a credible ally one cannot allow one's trading partners to be sacrificed to a man who threatens the stability of the Gulf. Oddly enough, in condemning Saddam's move against Kuwait there is another double standard: American policymakers seem to have forgotten how not too long ago the U.S. government sent troops to Panama to oust a drug dealer and Washington blatantly interfered in the politics of Nicaragua and sent the U.S. Navy to attempt an assassination of the Libyan leader, Muammar Qaddafi.

Why did American officials play down the poison gas attacks of the Iraqis during the Iran-Iraq war? Why did Washington ignore Saddam's threats or the fact that Iraq was perhaps only a few years, or months, away from achieving nuclear capabilities? That could easily be ascertained from U.S. satellite intelligence; doubtless the Bush administration must have known how close Saddam was to the ultimate weapon. Surely American officials realized that if Saddam were given a chance to develop and deploy nuclear arms, he would not hesitate to use them against Israel--his ultimate foe.

An example of this blindness in American thinking also appears in scholarly print. In 1988, Frederick W. Axelgard published a book for the Center for Strategic and International Studies (CSIS) in Washington, D.C.; it was titled *A New Iraq? - The Gulf War and Implications for U.S. Policy.* The preface to this study was solicited from and written by Hermann Frederick Eilts, former U.S. ambassador to Saudi Arabia and Egypt and later director of the Center for International Relations at Boston University. In the book Eilts mindlessly praises Axelgard and the latter's equally mindless pleas for a positive outlook toward Iraq. Axelgard emphasizes all the good things that Saddam Hussein did for the Shi'a and Kurdish minorities in Iraq. He states such things as attracting Shi'a members to the Ba'ath party, which also included channeling industrial development into the southern, Shi'a areas, symbolic religious gestures to the Shi'ites, the economic development of Kurdish areas, and land reform. He states that these Shi'ites were more loyal to the Iraqi leadership than to their Iranian co-religionists during the eight-year war. Axelgard also believes that the Kurds were so politically divided that they were not at all effective. He only briefly mentions how Iraqi Shi'ites were being arrested, expelled, or murdered by Saddam's secret police. Nor does he mention the punishment meted out to Kurdish separatists, the harsh resettlement campaigns, the use of chemical weapons against the Kurds, against their children, the razing of Kurdish villages, and the Turkish-Iraqi agreement that allowed either Turks or Iraqis to pursue Kurdish rebels into each other's territory. The impression one gets from Axelgard's analysis is that Saddam was essentially compelled to do what he did and that the Shi'ites and Kurds got what they deserved.[13] That an informed author could ignore the murder of innocent women and children and the use of terrorist tactics by a government on its own people is absolutely reprehensible.

The center for which Axelgard works, CSIS, is an American "think tank," that, with the exception perhaps of Walter Lacquer, in its Asian, Soviet, and Middle East section is known in the U.S. capital for its pervasive mediocrity. Consider a sample of Axelgard's writing: "Might not this leadership exert a lasting, stabilizing influence on Iraq and lift it out of its condition of perpetual tenuousness into the vitality of a full-fledged nation-state?"[14] Toward the end of the book, Axelgard gives both a summation of the Iraqi regime and a telling prognosis: "Saddam Hussein has injected moderation and pragmatism into a wide range of his external policies, from relations with the superpowers and the conservative Arab states of the Gulf to gestures of restraint and acceptance on the Arab-Israeli conflict"[15] and "after 40 years of volatility, realism may yet spawn a sustainable U.S. policy toward Iraq."[16]

I am not suggesting that Axelgard's analyses were carefully weighted as a determining factor in the minds of U.S. policymakers. But there was a minimal acceptance of this thesis by Washington. How could the U.S. government, staffed with some of the most brilliant political minds in the world, allow itself to follow such a policy prescription?

The answer, disturbingly enough, seems to come down to bare economics. Ever since the reestablishment of ties between the United States and Iraq in 1984, Iraq had been the largest importer of American rice and wheat. Not surprisingly, an unofficial pro-Iraqi lobby operated in Washington; its purpose was to keep relations between the two countries on a sound footing. In fact, at the height of the Gulf crisis, several representatives of America's wheat and rice farmers made a strong bid to prevent the imposition of sanctions against Iraq following its invasion of Iran.

Business contacts with Iraq were not just limited to the grain and arms trade. A number of very influential American companies founded the U.S.-Iraq Business Forum, which acted as a lobby group for Iraqi interests in Washington. Henry Kissinger's consulting firm, Kissinger Associates, was a member of this group, even though the former secretary of state later became very vocal about armed force against Iraq. Dozens of major corporations in the United States supplied Hussein with everything from food to computers to helicopters to, in Kissinger's case, economic advice. These companies, although headed by chairpersons who straddled the worlds of business and diplomacy, conveniently ignored the possible threat they must have known Iraq could pose to the world, in exchange for the almighty dollar. In exchange for oil and other goods, the companies made sure that Iraq received favorable credits and loan guarantees from the federal government. "Safeguarding these subsidies from congressional sanctions and federal bureaucracy was, from 1982 until August 1990, the *raison d'être* of the U.S.-Iraq Business Forum."[17] The group worked closely with the Iraqi embassy, and as a way of thanks, in 1985 Hussein made it mandatory for U.S. business interests to belong to the Forum if they wanted to do business with Iraq. An example of their blindness occurred in May 1988 during Hussein's brutal repression of the Kurds. The Business Forum sponsored a symposium on Iraq that was entirely made up of apologists for the Iraqi regime. During the resulting debate on the imposition of sanctions against Iraq, the Forum used its contacts to pressure the Reagan administration to oppose these sanctions.

PRELUDE TO INVASION

In the waning days of the hot month of July 1990, Saddam's propaganda machine was still saber-rattling; his forces were still massing on the Iraqi-Kuwaiti border. There did not seem to be the slightest evidence, however, that Saddam was massing elite units of the Republican Guard, not from Western embassy reports on the ground or from a bird's-eye view of the situation. Traffic on the Basra-Kuwait highway was unusually heavy. Everything else looked abnormally calm.

But the signals kept coming, sporadic at first, then somewhat feverishly. Israeli Mossad operatives were reporting to Yitzhak Shamir's cabinet that an invasion of Kuwait was imminent. There was information arriving from the U.S. National Security Agency (NSA) based on intelligence from satellite reconnaissance data and electronic monitoring (ELINT). These and American-manned Saudi AWACS aircraft as well as U.S. men-of-war sent out to patrol the northern waters of the Gulf on or around July 24, had been picking up signals between Baghdad and the Iraqi troops on the border.

Baghdad tried desperately to have everything as well camouflaged as possible. Saddam was carefully communicating with the forward positions of the Republican Guard not by radio, which could be easily detected by NSA's electronic eavesdropping, but by dispatch riders (simple couriers) and by field telephones hooked up by short cables. But that too was being penetrated by the United States. On Wednesday, August 1, there was a meeting at the White House where CIA head William Webster told President Bush, "They are ready; they will go."

Ironically, the evening before the *tête-à-tête* at the White House, Undersecretary of State John Kelly appeared at a congressional hearing and said that the United States was monitoring the situation and would help its friends in the Gulf. In the same breath he ambivalently reminded the congressmen that the United States had no defense treaties with any of the Arab Gulf states. He did not disclose, nor could he have known, the fact that the next day the American president would secretly be meeting with his CIA chief and that on the same day, August 1, there would be a parallel meeting in a sealed, debugged room at the Pentagon. Chairman of the Joint Chiefs of Staff (JCS) Colin Powell was quietly listening to an up-to-date report on the Gulf delivered by a heavy-set veteran of the Vietnam conflict, General Norman Schwarzkopf. The latter was in command of the U.S. Army's Central Command (USCENTCOM), a defense project that was successor to former president Jimmy Carter's Rapid Deployment Force. The USCENTCOM was in the Gulf primarily to protect the Arab oil fields after the fall of the Shah and the Soviet invasion of Afghanistan. No one expected the danger at that time to come from Iraq.

Kuwaiti intelligence was itself abreast of what was happening. Kuwait City, on the eve of the invasion, was a city of rumors. It breathed rumors, consumed only rumors. People were already beginning to leave in the hundreds of thousands for Jordan. The rich were flying out to London and Paris, from there to the United States. No one believed official press statements anymore. Rumor had it that secret meetings were taking place between Iraqi statesmen and their Kuwaiti counterparts. It was rumored that the al-Sabah ruling family was already anxious to give in to the Iraqi demands. It was feared that the United States would not come to the aid of Kuwait, not when it came down to the crunch. But what basis was there for all these rumors? The evidence was all circumstantial. But the rumors kept on coming.

On the night of July 31, the Iraqis and Kuwaitis were ready to meet to try and defuse the crisis in Jeddah. The Kuwaitis were desperate.

The countdown to the invasion had started. The Pentagon, the CIA, the American president, the Egyptian president, the Israelis, and the Kuwaitis themselves knew it was coming. The Jordanian king was most likely privy to it, as were a number of Palestinian leaders, perhaps George Habash, perhaps Yasser Arafat. The Saudis suspected something serious was afoot; there were countless Iraqi spies running loose in Riyadh, in Jedda, and along the whole Saudi coast, assessing American port defenses. There was no way of knowing how many Palestinians and Saudis were on the Baghdad payroll as agents, informers, saboteurs. The meeting with Colin Powell, General Schwarzkopf, and U.S. Defense Secretary Cheney, just 13 hours before the Iraqi invasion, revealed the inadequacy of American forces to stop the Iraqis if they attacked Kuwait. True, there was no contingency plan to stop Saddam. True, the Iraqi dictator could have rolled across Kuwait and Saudi Arabia in a matter of days. But he could never have brought it off without huge losses to his army and air force. The Americans were already in Saudi Arabia. U.S. naval vessels were patrolling the Gulf waters, and there was a bomber base on Diego

Garcia in the Indian Ocean. The Americans were not sitting ducks against Iraqi armor and French-built Exocet missiles. Whatever initial victory Saddam was able to score, it would not have taken more than one month to bring effective air power against him. The Pentagon nevertheless pretended that it was being hard-pressed. It was ready to inflame the crisis.

The Jeddah meeting opened in an atmosphere of great expectations; it was all one-sided, though. The Kuwaiti team, headed by the same craven prime minister, Sheikh Sa'ad al-Abdallah, came to meet with Saddam's deputy, Izzat Ibrahim, a greasy Ba'athist "yes-man," with no authorization to make any deal. He was merely sent there by his master to stall for time. The Kuwaiti prince of the blood was alternately abject and defensive. "We have evidence," he declared in a pitifully meek voice, "that you want to invade us."

Unequivocally, the Kuwaiti prime minister agreed to write off Iraqi debts (totaling $14 or $15 billion) to Kuwait and to lease Warbah Island to Iraq. The mousy Izzat Ibrahim also asked for Bubiyan Island, whereupon the Kuwaiti stammered, surprised to hear Saddam's delegate was so forceful, and rudely refused.[18] Ibrahim launched a tirade, demanding oil-pumping rights and a further $10 billion from the Kuwaitis. The meeting quickly adjourned and reconvened the following morning.

On the morning of the 1st of August, only three men came to the negotiating table: the two official envoys in the presence of Prince Sa'ud al-Faisal, the Saudi foreign minister, who chaired the meeting. Ibrahim immediately feigned a headache and expressed a wish to retire to his room. Both the Saudi and the Kuwaiti pleaded with him to stay. But Ibrahim was not really in a position to continue the discussions. He was carrying out Saddam's orders, that's all!

The future scenario had already been charted by Baghdad. Saddam knew that Kuwait was doomed. Saddam could now gloat over it. He was determined to conquer. But he too was destined to fall into an insidious trap. There were people in the Pentagon who were hoping he would make that plunge. Afterward they would ensnare him.

NOTES

1.   Abel Darwish and Gregory Alexander, *Unholy Babylon* (London: Victor Gollancz Ltd., 1991), p. 4.

2.   There were allegations that Bazoft had been spying for Israel and Britain and for this purpose he was allegedly investigating Iraq's missile program.

3.   Judith Miller and Laurie Mylroie, *Saddam Hussein and the Crisis in the Gulf* (New York: Times Books, 1990), p. 12.

4. The U.S. State Department called the threat "inflammatory, outrageous and irresponsible."

5. Iraqi embassy press release in Washington, D.C., September 1990.

6. Note from Tariq Aziz to the secretary-general of the Arab League, July 15, 1990. Reported in Pierre Salinger and Eric Laurent, *Secret Dossier: The Hidden Agenda Behind the Gulf War*, trans. by Howard Curtis (New York: Penguin, 1991).

7. *The Economist*, July 21, 1990, p. 22.

8. Transcript released by the Iraqi embassy in Washington and published in the *New York Times*.

9. *New York Times*, June 12, 1990.

10. *Washington Post*, July 30, 1990.

11. See Hedrick Smith, *The Power Game: How Washington Works* (New York: Ballantine Books, 1988), p. 592. One of the leading American stars in investigative journalism, Bob Woodward, in his book *The Commanders* (New York: Simon and Schuster, 1991) tells us President George Bush short-circuited the entire decision-making operation.

12. *Time*, March 11, 1991, p. 49.

13. Axelgard pays scant attention to Saddam Hussein's practice of abducting and torturing the children of the Iraqi Kurdish families. For a good account of the Iraqi torture practices, see *Middle East Watch, Human Rights in Iraq* (New Haven: Yale University Press, 1990).

14. Frederick W. Axelgard, *A New Iraq?--The Gulf War and Implications for U.S. Policy* (New York: Praeger, 1988), pp. 47-48.

15. Ibid.

16. Ibid., p. 91.

17. Joe Conason, "The Iraq Lobby: Kissinger, the Business Forum & Co.," in Micah L. Sifry and Christopher Cert, eds., *The Gulf War Reader: History, Documents, Opinions* (Toronto: Times Books, 1991), p. 80. Originally appeared in the *New Republic* on October 1, 1990.

18. The Kuwaiti version of the meeting appeared in the Egyptian daily *Al-Mosàwar*, on the basis of an interview with Sheikh Sabah al-Ahmad, September 5, 1990.

5

Squaring Off

SADDAM HUSSEIN'S STATE OF MIND

The curious spectator to this continuing story can be likened to a dedicated patron of a reputable theater. Seated open-mouthed in a remote back row, he is watching an old thriller. While the rest of the audience sits silently, our spectator studies the scene with awe. Face contorted, looking nervous, suspicious, vigilant, he wants to shout a warning to the innocent girl on the screen--to warn her, as a groping hand reaches out through a panel in the wall to seize her by the throat. But will shouting be of any use? Has this picture not already been shot? Is it therefore not too late and the event beyond anyone's control?

It is a complete mystery how Saddam Hussein was able to neutralize Iran while he prepared to attack Kuwait. Was Iran no longer a major threat? My own guess is that senior military officers of the Iraqi army and air force were concerned that Iraq would be involved in a wide-scale military confrontation with the United States if Iraq were to go ahead with the invasion of Kuwait. So the Ba'athist leadership, collectively this time, decided to make amends with Iran. The mystery is the precise date of the approach to Iran for a peace treaty. A mystery, too, is the degree of Iranian cooperation in the Iraqi plans. Were the Iranians privy to Iraq's overall strategy months before? If Teheran did acquiesce in any plans, it was understandable why it would do so. There was no love lost between Iran and Kuwait: Kuwait supported Iraq against Iran during the eight-year bloodletting.

Iraq's peace offer was accepted by Teheran without the slightest ceremony. It called for a peace treaty, complete withdrawal of all troops from occupied territories, exchange of prisoners of war, and acceptance of the Algiers boundary demarcation. The terms of this accord were most favorable to Iran. Teheran got everything back that it had lost in the war. The only other source of disagreement between these erstwhile combatants was the Iraqi-based People's Mujahedin of Iran, which seeks to overthrow the Iranian government. Repatriation of war prisoners was never considered a hindrance in the peace process. Saddam was determined to get all his POWs back from Iran to help fulfil his next pan-Arab adventure.[1]

During the early morning hours of August 2, Iraqi tanks rumbled across the border of Kuwait and quickly crushed all armed resistance. On the 8th, Baghdad officially annexed Kuwait as part of its 19th province, an extension of Basra. Iraqi newspapers reported that the Kuwaiti government had been overthrown by Kuwaiti revolutionaries, who had asked Iraq for assistance. By that date the U.N. Security Council, by a 14 to 1 margin, had condemned the invasion and adopted Resolution 661 which placed trade sanctions on Iraq. No member of the United Nations was to be allowed to trade with the Iraqis. The immediate Western reaction was one of outrage. The United States, in particular, feared that Saddam Hussein would go further and attack Saudi Arabia, the principal American ally in the region. Washington, London, and Paris immediately froze Iraqi and Kuwaiti assets, halting imports from Iraq, and Saudi Arabia stopped all arms deliveries to Hussein's regime and closed its Iraqi oil pipeline. Ankara acceded to a similar request and closed its Iraqi oil pipeline. The United Nations approved the deployment of a security force to the Gulf to enforce its sanctions.

The Iraqis pushed their armor and artillery right up to the Saudi border. The first week of August was stiflingly hot, the midsummer nights balmy. Kuwait City was in utter chaos. The ruling family of Kuwait and the other very wealthy Kuwaitis had fled, leaving the Iraqi soldiers to go on a rampage. Baghdad immediately issued an order to terrorize the population into submission. Booty could be freely taken by the invading army.

From house to house the Iraqi regulars moved into the affluent districts of the Kuwaiti capital. They ransacked all the rooms, gutted the new libraries, broke into spacious vaults containing foreign currency, searched for precious jewels and stones, and hunted down Kuwaiti army officers to the last man. Perhaps the most heart-rending image that we have carried with us in this war was the report that 300 premature babies were thrown on the floor and left to die when Iraqi soldiers carted off their incubators from one of Kuwait's major hospitals. But hindsight reveals that this story was planted by the 15-year old daughter of the Kuwaiti Ambassador to the United States in order to make the American public more responsive to Saddam's atrocities. The soldiers also removed all the computers from a technical training college.[2]

Not content with this outrage, Iraqi army thieves turned upon their victims with an unspeakable barbarism. They captured 400 disguised Kuwaiti soldiers and slaughtered them all. Into the cellar of a house belonging to a prominent Kuwaiti prince of the blood they herded non-Muslim domestic women and young Filipino serving maids, some of whom were the prince's mistresses. The women were kept in the dark cellar all night. At daybreak, they were given water, ordered to undress, and wash, and then mercilessly whipped and raped by the cruel assailants.[3] The menfolk were led into a courtyard and decapitated one by one, their hands clasped behind their backs as the ax fell. The bedlam and bloody orgy only ended when 27 women were brought before the firing squad on the afternoon of the next day.

With hate-ridden words and gestures, the Iraqi secret police, having cornered a prominent Kuwaiti banker in his villa, had his eyes gouged out--while they were yelling out to him how disdainful it was to be robbing the Arab people and to rule in the name of the American and English imperialists. In full view of his family, the man was quartered with a chain saw. His limbs and torso were mounted on stakes; his head was hurled into a nearby gutter. Manor houses along the Kuwaiti coast were attacked for more than booty; wives and daughters of the wealthy merchants were raped, cattle were seized, stores of grain and rice confiscated, all valuables taken, and the title deeds burned. Roving bands of Iraqi hit squads went on burning, looting, and massacring. Sometimes they took bribes; sometimes they fought sporadic skirmishes with members of the resistance. But whatever resistance was left was eventually forced to go underground.

Saddam Hussein arrived in Kuwait toward the end of August to inspect his army's sinister work. This was not the first time he had visited the Kuwaiti capital; he had been wined and feted by Kuwait dignitaries in the past, men whom he held in contempt. So he had his own reasons to think that what was happening to Kuwait was a good thing. Saddam regarded Kuwait as opulence itself. He had traveled and explored at least one other Arab country in his lifetime. He had been to Cairo and Alexandria in Egypt. He had seen footage of Palestinians living in the squalor of refugee camps. He had visited Beirut, many years ago, before the civil war completely despoiled that city.

When looking at Kuwait City he must have witnessed the local contrasts of luxury with the hunger and the misery of poorer Arab cities. It probably filled him with pity, anger, and disgust. Was he so callous that he could not feel for the Arab poor? Could he not feel the corruption of civil servants in most Arab capitals? He remembered the fashionable districts of Alexandria, for example, where he saw the orgies of European chauvinism. In the poorer sections of Cairo he saw small, crowded lanes, nests of destitution, where narrow and crooked streets swerved and disappeared behind dark and foreboding corners. The shanties were lice-infested, rat-eaten.

Beggars trudged over these rutted passages, their feet wrapped in rags or left naked, their bodies bloated grotesquely by famine. Children lay in the streets or huddled in burlap gowns to protect them from the night. Arab children slept in tattered blankets that doubled as coats draped over their shoulders. Before the first rain, the urchins and old men of the alleyways would have their soles raked with open wounds. At one of the French hotels in Beirut, Saddam remembered seductive and well-fed Arab beauties who arrived at their trysting places to meet generous foreigners and high-born Maronite officers. In Beirut's destitute quarters he saw half-dressed, half-veiled harlots standing in doorways or walking the sewage-infested sidewalks with bloated torsos and gnarled hands. A wretched humanity was living on unpaved side streets.

Ali Hassan al-Majid, Saddam's cousin and the Iraqi minister of local government, who had been in charge of the Iraqi suppression of the Kurds, was placed in charge of Kuwait and was told to 'Iraqise' the emirate by repeating the Kurdistan experiment. A Kuwaiti underground movement, of no more than 60 groups, sprang up but was summarily dealt with by the Iraqi occupiers. In fact, members of the Kuwaiti resistance claimed that Iranians helped to train them in the use of explosives. The Kuwaiti government-in-exile smuggled nearly $100 million into the country to be used for bribes and to buy necessities.

On September 18, a large number of Kuwaitis were rounded up in what was thought to have been the first step in drafting them into the Iraqi army. On October 1, the Iraqis hanged five Filipinos who worked for the Kuwaiti underground. Freed hostages gave reports of Kuwaitis being mutilated or murdered for harboring Westerners.[4]

We must stop here and ask ourselves: What was Saddam Hussein's real ambition with respect to Kuwait? Was it really the oil? Was it the extension of the Iraqi shoreline or nothing short of outright annexation? Two days after Saddam Hussein annexed Kuwait, he went on record as saying that his withdrawal from Kuwait was linked to the Palestinian issue. Iraq was ready to accept U.N. Resolution 660 if Israel would comply with U.N. Resolution 242 and withdraw from Arab land.

The Iraqi ruler hinted that a Mideast conference should be held to settle the issue of a Palestinian state. He also shrewdly hinted that if the Allies in Saudi Arabia attacked him, he would involve Israel in a war by attacking it. If the Israelis retaliated, which he expected, Saddam knew that many of the Arab troops in the U.S.-led multinational force would refuse to fight against Iraq. His announcements did not fall on deaf ears, neither in Egypt nor in Syria, and this policy of linkage was getting enormous popular support among the citizens of Jordan and from their Hashemite King. Was Saddam ready to withdraw from Kuwait at a moment's notice?

In the long run, Saddam probably had no intention of remaining in Kuwait. If he could get the Israelis to suddenly change their minds about the West Bank or risk a major war, he would go down in the annals of Mideast history as the greatest Arab of all time. Kuwait could be used as a trade-off. To the outside observer it all looked politically naive. It *was* politically naive. Or else it was the play of a consummate diplomatic strategist, who takes a chance, procrastinates as long as he can, rallies the whole Arab world to his side, and then quietly withdraws from Kuwait. In many ways, Iraq was still signalling to the United States, through its ambassador and through King Hussein of Jordan, that it could still be the guardian of U.S. interests in the region, that the Iraqi army could and would withdraw.

While the Iraqis were making these overtures--and this is another indication that Saddam was not spoiling for another war and had no intention of remaining in Kuwait--his elite troops were stripping Kuwait threadbare of every precious item. In the first two weeks, they robbed Kuwait of every advanced computer. Everything that could be dismantled was put on trucks. For days the lorries hauled back to Baghdad research laboratories, gold bullion, German and Japanese automobiles, spare parts, traffic lights, and the emir's thoroughbred horses. By mid-December, the Iraqis had looted approximately 45 billion dollars' worth of goods.[5]

U.S. POLICY TURNS AGAINST HUSSEIN

American decision makers realized that if the United States did not get involved in a new Gulf war, if they did not now stop the Iraqi dictator, Israel might pre-empt Iraqi threats and attack directly. This might have drawn the entire Arab world into a conflict with Israel. Israel, if pressed, might unhesitatingly use nuclear weapons, and the resulting escalation would lead to a world war. Besides, Iraq was itself only a few months, at worst perhaps one or two years, away from possessing a nuclear bomb. Nuclear proliferation in the Middle East was like playing with dynamite. A major conflagration could interrupt the world's, if not necessarily America's, oil supply.[6]

This delicate situation in the Gulf was throwing the U.S. foreign policy establishment into a state of pandemonium. By the beginning of November, three agencies in Washington were trying to work out some policy: the White House, the State Department, and the Pentagon.

President Bush wanted to be closely involved in any war decision. Sending troops and equipment to the Gulf "had its own logic," opined a New York political columnist later on.[7] The talk about sanctions and diplomacy were "necessary political precursors of war."[8] It was also necessary to stall for time, just as Saddam was doing, so that the United States and its allies could build up their forces in the Gulf region. Bush realized what the long-range implications of such a war would be. Many in the administration were warning the president about the dangers of destroying Iraq completely, about leaving a vacuum there. Who would fill that vacuum? The Kurds? The Shi'ites? In his press conferences, Bush ended up speaking about oil, about Iraq's possession of chemical weapons, and about the efforts to develop nuclear weapons. For the first time, he broached the subject of establishing a "new world order" in the wake of the Cold War. He wanted to solve this issue without a protracted war in an election year. Consequently, Bush could not fathom Saddam Hussein. When news of Iraqi atrocities in Kuwait reached him, Bush found it convenient to be judgmental. In a letter to college students, the president wrote that there was much in the world "washed in shades of gray." He added: "But not the brutal aggression of Saddam Hussein; it's black and white."[9]

So George Bush began personalizing the issue with Saddam Hussein. The president was shown on television, swaggering like Clint Eastwood in a "make-my-day" show of defiance, and loudly proclaiming that Saddam was "going to get his ass kicked." Of course, some of the president's advisors--not all--were urging him on in a course of action that ruled out diplomacy. The others probably expected economic sanctions to work against Iraq. The more hawkish attitude prevailed: it was the only way of ridding Saddam of his offensive weapons and his war-making capacity.

James Baker and his own advisors in the State Department were clearly in favor of a negotiated settlement. There was the possibility of Baker leaving for Baghdad to meet with Hussein. But the idea was scuttled by George Bush. In mid-December, a peace initiative was made by Algeria--the Saudis concurred; the Iraqis agreed. Again the White House refused. The U.S. president unambiguously stated that there would be no give on a Mideast peace conference and that "there can be no face-saving"--the president was "not in a negotiating mood."[10]

What worried the Bush administration more than anything else was that most Europeans, most Arabs for that matter, were willing to go along with a partial Iraqi withdrawal from Kuwait. That "peaceful solution" would have at least left the disputed islands and the Rumaila oil fields in Baghdad's hands. Saddam's military might would have remained intact. Bush's supporters were fearful that Saddam might accept the U.N. deadline for withdrawal and thus make it impossible for the United States to go to war. This is very common to human nature: the public is not really for war; it decries war, cries for a peaceful solution. The government publicly goes through the motions of seeking peace by diplomacy and dialogue. These are only words, however. Secretly most people are for the war. Most believe it to be the only possible solution. This is the line of reasoning that also prevailed in the American military establishment--the Pentagon.

There were other domestic reasons why this war was considered propitious for most Americans. The United States was going through a severe recession. Unemployment was high. Violence was rife in American cities.

Hunger was not unusual in the streets; homelessness, too. Banks were failing. The government's lackluster performance in implementing badly needed social programs was criticized. Bush was generally regarded as an ineffectual wimp with regard to domestic policy. With a successful war, a popular war, Bush's popularity was bound to be restored.

Another compelling reason why the American leadership needed this Gulf war was the nation's failure in Vietnam 20 years before. There was considerable damage done to the American psyche. Americans would re-member that conflict as the first major war the United States lost. Fighting in Vietnam had been unpopular, both at home and abroad. Four million men had taken part in it, and nearly 100,000 men deserted; a further 100,000 fled to Sweden or to Canada to escape the draft. Thousands faked illness and mental disability or wilfully maimed themselves; others joined either the reserves or the National Guard. Many of the survivors developed some form of Post-Traumatic Stress Disorder.

Furthermore, the Communist threat, one of the excuses for the war, was still unchecked in Vietnam and the U.S. promise to help the South Vietnamese came to nothing. The morale of the American nation was broken. There were protests at home; the country built a barrier between itself and the military. The United States went into a state of collective amnesia. Vietnam meant a loss of innocence.

Following the American defeat in Vietnam, the rest of Indochina (Cambodia and Laos) quickly fell to Communist incursions. The war led to strong popular opposition to military intervention abroad. The American government then turned to covert and proxy wars by supplying materials, military assistance, and advisors to troubled spots throughout the world, from Afghanistan to Iran and from Central America to Lebanon.

The American embassy personnel were taken hostage in Teheran af-ter the Shah fell from power. President Jimmy Carter agreed to a mission to rescue the American hostages. Washington was going to try to do what the Israelis succeeded in doing at Entebbe. In April 1980, a joint navy and air force team was put together under the code name "Eagle Claw." Its mission was to fly into Iran and rescue the hostages. On April 24 the exercise began, and it just as unexpectedly fell apart the next day--several rescue helicopters crashed, leaving eight dead and three wounded. The Iranians were thus able to obtain helicopter technology, weapons, maps, and secret documents, which they used for propaganda purposes.

The failure of this mission did nothing to restore American pride in their military and, at least partly, led to the defeat of Jimmy Carter in the elections of 1980. It also resulted in the resignation of Cyrus Vance, Carter's secretary of state, who had opposed the adventure from the beginning. The American scholar James A. Bill cogently summed up the U.S. public's embarrassment when he wrote: "In short, the American eagle left a broken claw in the deserts of Iran in April 1980."[11]

The next minor military skirmish took place on August 19, 1981, when the U. S. Navy deliberately provoked two Libyan pilots into engaging two U.S. Navy aircraft. Both Libyan planes were destroyed. At the time, President Ronald Reagan condemned Libyan-sponsored terrorism and used this excuse to provoke a confrontation. The American public seemed somewhat apathetic, especially when it was revealed that the navy exercises in the Gulf of Sidra were deliberately staged in an area claimed by Libya as territorial waters.

Next the U.S. military became involved in the protection of Palestinian and Syrian troops from Israeli Defense Forces in Lebanon. Between August 1982 and February 1984, American marines were stationed in Beirut. The venture seemed doomed from the very start. A number of marines were killed in small skirmishes. The U.S. embassy in Lebanon was bombed on April 18, 1983. Finally, in what proved to be one of the most humiliating setbacks for the U.S. Marines, suicide bombers blew up the marine barracks in Beirut on October 23, 1983. In that incident, 255 U.S. Marines were killed and 168 wounded. U.S. forces were withdrawn from Lebanon by March 30, 1984, having failed in all their objectives. Again, America was outraged and its people further alienated from the military.

The "Urgent Fury" mission to invade the small Caribbean island of Grenada in early November of 1983 took some of the sting away from the public's sense of betrayal. Ostensibly, the invasion was an exercise to stop the spread of Marxist revolutions throughout the Caribbean and protect threatened American lives. The American people were told that Grenada could be used as a staging area for Cuban and Soviet flights to their interests in Africa. They were also informed that the Organization of Eastern Caribbean States had asked the United States to intervene and had sent security contingents from Antigua, Dominica, Saint Lucia, Saint Vincent, Barbados, and Jamaica. The invasion took place from October 25 to November 2, with American forces staying on until December 4. All in all, 11 U.S. Army soldiers were killed, with 106 wounded, 7 navy personnel were killed, with 7 wounded, and 2 pilots were wounded. Feeling the part of world defenders once again, the public was confused and angered when rifts appeared between the United States and the major European allies, the South Americans, and the Commonwealth countries. But, for the first time, there was a flicker of pride. Capturing the euphoric mood of the country over finally winning something, a character in Mark Alan Stamaty's political cartoon *Washingtoon* quipped, "Gosh! If a small-scale invasion feels this good, imagine how great a war would feel!"[12]

The next military operation took place in 1986 after Colonel Qaddafi's Libya was linked with terrorist actions and the deaths of American servicemen in an explosion in a bar in West Germany. President Ronald Reagan, a long-time opponent of Qaddafi's regime, ordered a raid on Tripoli and

Benghazi in what many considered an officially sanctioned assassination attempt on Qaddafi. "Operation El Dorado Canyon" began on April 14 when U.S. Air Force aircraft took off from their bases in Britain. On April 15, these aircraft, along with navy aircraft, attacked targets in Benghazi and Tripoli. Several Libyan civilians were killed or injured, including Qaddafi's adopted daughter and two of his sons. The American public accepted this action as a curt message to terrorists, but America was also eager to show a mailed clout in the Middle East.

Under "Operation Staunch," the U.S. Navy undertook to protect merchant ships and oil tankers along with British, French, and Italian commercial vessels during the Iran-Iraq war. One of the American warships, the USS *Stark*, was attacked by an Iraqi jet firing an Exocet missile on May 17, 1987. Iraq claimed the attack was a mistake. U.S. crewmen were killed. To prevent such an act from reoccurring, the captain of the USS *Vincennes* ordered an Iranian airbus to be shot down when it appeared that it was on a suicide mission.

It was only with the 1989 invasion of Panama that the Americans regained their international pride. "Operation Just Cause" showed the United States that they could succeed in a war-like situation. With the ouster of General Manuel Noriega, the drug kingpin of Panamanian politics, American public opinion turned toward the military, the government, and its foreign-policy considerations again. Panama prepared the way for "Desert Shield" and "Desert Storm" by allowing Americans a renewed sense of pride in their military, now badly needed in a post-Vietnam America.

ENTER NORMAN SCHWARZKOPF

America also needed, and received, an all-American hero--army general H. Norman Schwarzkopf. He was already the commander of USCENTCOM, which meant that he was the commander in chief responsible for the Middle East and Southwest Asia. He appeared as *deus ex machina*, more so than the secretary of defense, Dick Cheney, and the chairman of the JCS, Colin Powell.

Schwarzkopf had all the prerequisite credentials for a hero: a former West Point football player, a larger-than-life personality, and a battle-hardened veteran of two tours of duty in Vietnam. He commanded the respect and admiration of the men serving under him.

But the burly soldier was a terror as a boss; no matter, the media happily endeared him to the public as a "gentle homebody" who goes fishing with the kids, fondles his pet snakes, plays Santa Claus at Christmas, or sits by a warm hearth scratching his favorite dog behind the ears. Americans nurtured themselves with these wholesome images, and few negative words, if any, could be said about this man.[13] Schwarzkopf

was without any doubt an excellent soldier, his excessive weight notwith-
standing, in an American army that was the technological wonder of the
world.

Schwarzkopf had taken up his command of USCENTCOM on November 3, 1988. It has been suggested by many writers that the general had
studied Saddam's character very well, that he knew the Iraqi to be a
ruthless ruler. It has also been suggested that Schwarzkopf had initiated
contingency plans in the Persian Gulf comprising the three services of the
JCS. Such plans involve strategic and tactical operations, communications, command and control, logistics, psychological warfare, search and
rescue, and special operations.

If there really was a contingency plan for American forces in anticipa-
tion of an Iraqi invasion of Kuwait, such would have been the normal
practice whoever happened to be designated the commander of USCENT-
COM. The final decisions would have had to be made at the level of the
JCS, not by General Schwarzkopf himself. That there was some U.S. contingency plan in the wake of the Iran-Iraq war should not be doubted,
however. One account has it that Schwarzkopf and his own staff had
"completed a computerized war game (CPX, Command Post Exercise)" in
July of 1990--one month before Saddam sent his troops into Kuwait.[14]
Another account maintains that the chairman of the JCS, Colin Powell,
asked Norman Schwarzkopf to evaluate the Iraqi troop buildup and
ordered Schwarzkopf to draft a two-tiered plan for possible U.S. responses
to any Iraqi move against Kuwait. Apparently, it was Schwarzkopf who was
the first to advocate an air war. The general reportedly said his motives
were simple:

> One, it's a target-rich environment--easy to see things. Secondly,
> Iraq has no experience operating under air attack. Three, we
> have sophisticated munitions with more precision than ever be-
> fore. Four, there could be quite a significant morale effect on the
> Iraqis in the rear who have never been subjected to danger in
> the past.[15]

Now where President Bush stood in the military preparations for war
is uncertain. The president could not afford a protracted war against Iraq:
American casualties would be too high. But he was compelled to give a
free hand to the Pentagon. More than this, he authorized a top-secret
voice communications link between Pentagon operations center and Israeli
Defense Force headquarters. This secure line was given the code name
"Hammer Rick" and was used to pass the very latest and best intelligence
to the Israelis about possible attacks against Israel.[16] In any event,
whatever action was decided upon or carried out by Schwarzkopf, it had
to have the imprimatur of the American president and the JCS. It will be

interesting to learn what Schwarzkopf has to say about all this in his published memoirs.

Iraqis themselves were not very well prepared by their leadership for the war. Only in mid-December were Iraqis told to build bomb shelters and the Iraqi ministries told to prepare for an attack. Massive civil defense drills were held in the days and hours before the beginning of the war. Iraq virtually blacked out all sensitive news so that its people did not know what they were up against. It is not certain but sometime before the actual air war began, U.S. agents introduced a 'virus' into several Iraqi computers that disabled Baghdad's communications with the Iraqi Air Force Command system. Iraq's planes were virtually useless.

WORLD WAR III VERSUS WORLD WAR I

But the Western media--true to the ways of unprofessional reporting and sensationalized journalism--fed the public with stories of 50,000 American body bags. Newspapers depicted Iraqi fighting discipline comparable to that of Roman legionnaires. Saddam's artillery was like the Red Army's. Frightening! Above all, there was the nightmare of chemical weapons. The world was nervously holding its breath. The U.S. military establishment, almost conspiratorially, fed these delusions to the world public.

Nothing was further from the truth. The Iraqis may not have been outnumbered in personnel; they were, however, hopelessly outgunned. Their training and professionalism could hardly be compared to that of the Allies. Pitted against American infantry and their rapid-movement tactics, the Iraqis did not stand a chance. Iraqi commanders knew they were vastly inferior to the Western coalition forces. Plots on Saddam Hussein's life by Iraqi army officers were discovered.

From the time when Desert Shield (the U.S. military buildup) began until Desert Storm (the U.S.-led operation to liberate Kuwait) was launched, a buildup of weapons took place. On its side, Iraq had an army numbering approximately 955,000 with 480,000 reserves (of which about 200,000 were stationed in Kuwait itself). Most of these men were combat veterans, having recently lived through the Iran-Iraq war. The elite troops, who were kept away from the front to be used in emergencies, included six divisions of the Republican Guard, headed by Hussein Kamel Hassan, Hussein's son-in-law. These elite armored, infantry and special-operations troops, up to 150,000 men, were intensely loyal to Hussein himself. In fact, they were paid double wages and had free housing and cars. The Iraqi forces in Kuwait would rely on an extensive network of mine fields, earth berms, razor wire, and trenches designed to make an enemy frontal assault as fruitlessly bloody as the British Somme offensive of 1916.

The Allied forces numbered in the following: the United States sent in the Third Army, which consisted of approximately 250,000 to 300,000 troops (comprising approximately 60 percent of all of the Allied troops); Saudi Arabia had about 75,000 troops; the United Kingdom 30,000; Canada 1,700; Egypt 35,000; France 5,500; Syria 20,000 with 8-10,000 committed; Kuwait 7,000; Pakistan 5,000; and other countries sent small contingents (Morocco, Czechoslovakia, Honduras, Bangladesh, the United Arab Emirates, Qatar, Bahrain, Niger, Senegal, Poland, Hungary, etc.) numbering approximately 10,000; giving a total of over 400,000 troops. The American and English troops were all well trained. The American military to begin with is an all-volunteer force with possibly the highest education and training level in U.S. history. In addition to this, U.S. Army Special Forces and Delta Force commandos as well as the U.S. Navy Seals (Sea, Air, Land) were ready to move in behind Iraqi lines.

Best estimates gave Iraq approximately 4,000 Soviet-built tanks (including T-72s, T-54s, T-55s, and T-62s). However, no one could have been sure of their serviceability after the Iran-Iraq war. They had no replacements from the Soviet Union. They had only enough armored personnel carriers to transport about 10 percent of their troops; most were Soviet-built BTR series. They had significant numbers of towed and self-propelled artillery, but again the issue of maintenance and ammunition supply came into question. However, they had large numbers of non-sophisticated Air Defense Artillery and were equipped with Franco-German HOT and Milan anti-tank missiles and AT-3 Sagger and AT-4 Spigot anti-tank missiles. They also had approximately 2,700 pieces of artillery and 700 plus Surface to Air Missiles (SAMs), which were the only things that could have posed a major threat to Allied air power. The only horrific weapon the Iraqis could employ was more a weapon of terror than effective combat. It was the modified Soviet Scud-B missile, the "al-Hussein," which, although inaccurate, contained conventional high explosives. The Scud could have been modified even further to launch biological and chemical warheads. But the Iraqis did not develop it to that point. Their electronic delivery system was still in its infancy. The Scuds could be fired from both fixed and mobile launchers. But the fixed launchers could easily be spotted from the air and knocked out. Last but not least, the Iraqis possessed some Exocet missiles, but these could only be fired from helicopters and jet fighters. Baghdad had about 330 helicopters, of which only about 50 could carry Exocets. The fighter or helicopter would still have to come fairly close to its target to make the kill. Otherwise it could be shot out of the air.

The total air superiority of the Allied, particularly American, air force could be devastatingly effective against the Iraqis. The Allies controlled about 1,100 aircraft and approximately 100,000 personnel with contingents from the United States, Saudi Arabia, the United Kingdom, France, Canada, Italy, and the Gulf states. Most of the fighters were very modern and advanced, while only some of the pilots had had combat experience. Some of the most sophisticated were the American F15, F16, F18 and F117 fighters. The Americans' long-range B-52G bombers could carry approximately 40,000 pounds of conventional bombs and had the advantage of being able to fly at over 50,000 feet. They also could attack Iraqi positions from bases as far away as Diego Garcia in the Indian Ocean, Spain, Britain, and Louisiana.

The Iraqis' navy was of little threat to the Allied navies except for their small missile boats. The Allied navy included aircraft carriers, battleships, guided missile cruisers, destroyers, frigates, corvettes, and fast patrol boats plus support ships, assault ships, mine countermeasure vessels, and submarines. There were approximately 75,000 to 80,000 personnel from the United States, the United Kingdom, Australia, Canada, Argentina, Belgium, Denmark, Norway, France, Greece, Italy, the Netherlands, Germany, Spain, Portugal, the USSR, Turkey, Saudi Arabia, and the Gulf states. As well, the U.S. Navy Seals were used to stake out the beaches of Kuwait for possible landing sites and landed there in hovercraft.

The use of poison gas dates back to the use of mustard gas against the Allied trenches in World War I as well as the use of gas by the Japanese against the Chinese in the 1930s and by Italy in Ethiopia. The use of chemical arms was outlawed by the 1925 Geneva Protocol. Although Iraq signed, along with most countries, the Biological and Toxin Weapons Convention in 1972, this convention only prohibits the use of chemical weapons, not the manufacture or stockpiling of such armaments. It was estimated that Iraq had 2,000 to 4,000 tons stockpiled. Among the most virulent strains are mustard gas, which was used during World War I and causes skin blisters and burns the lungs. It can be fatal in high doses. Iraq had Sarin and Tabun, both of which can paralyze the central nervous system and cause death. The Iraqis have also stockpiled biological weapons, such as anthrax.

However, chemical weapons are unreliable. They must be dropped either from low-flying planes (Iraq quickly lost that option once the air war began) or in bombs, artillery shells, missiles, and rockets (although this would have to involve a large concentration of bombs, and so forth) which would have to land very accurately. There were reports that the Iraqis were using chemical components in their mines that, when detonated, released clouds of gas. But the Iraqis would have to pinpoint the Allies without communications or air reconnaissance. Also, the wind that blew during the war would have blown the gas back onto the Iraqi positions. Besides, all of the Allied troops carried gas masks and chemical gear.

Moreover, the Allies could take advantage of their spy satellites, sophisticated jamming devices, and night-fighting equipment. The Iraqis also had a series of underground bunkers that they used to house their airplanes and soldiers. These were particularly difficult to find.

The Allies also used American AWACS (Airborne Warning and Control System), which were highly sophisticated radar jets; ECM (Electronic Counter-Measures), which blinded radar; LANTIRN (Low Altitude Navigation and Targeting InfraRed for Night); JSTARS (Joint Surveillance and Target Attack Radar System), which was used to track ground targets; smart bombs, which were highly accurate and were guided by radar, laser, infrared light, or television; TLAM (Tactical Land Attack Missile), which included Tomahawks; CBU (Cluster Bombs), little bombs that spread over a large area and then explode; HAVE NAP, which are Israeli-made missiles with built-in cameras that pilots can direct straight to the target; IRCM (InfraRed CounterMeasures), which masked tanks, guns, aircraft, and so forth, from heat-seeking sensors, missiles, or rockets); and LCAC (Landing-Craft Air-Cushion hovercraft), which can be used to bring marines and their equipment ashore.

The United States used the opportunity presented by this war to try out new high-tech weapons in actual combat situations. One was the E-8A JSTARS radar plane, which was a surveillance jet that could spot moving or stationary targets deep within Iraq using new radar technology that sees over the horizon. The Tomahawk II cruise missile, a ship- or submarine-launched, computer-guided missile with devastating accuracy, would be used very effectively. The Patriot air-defense missile system was the nearest thing to "Star Wars" technology that was unrivalled in the world's arms inventory. It knocked nearly every Scud missile launched at Israel and Saudi Arabia out of the air. The F-117A "Stealth" fighter-bomber is an attack jet capable of devastating surprise attacks because it can reach targets without being spotted by air-defense radar systems. The A-10 Thunderbolt attack fighter is a tank killer used in support of Allied ground troops. The AH64 Apache helicopter, another tank killer designed to fight in all weather, day or night. The Allies also had a sophisticated satellite network that gave them very valuable information for directing their armies.[17] All in all, the United States sent in 75 percent of its active tactical airplanes, 42 percent of its tanks, 46 percent of its Marines, 37 percent of its army, and 46 percent of its aircraft carriers.[18]

The Allies had been acutely embarrassed by circulated reports about the help they had given Iraq during and after the Iran-Iraq war. Being the lesser of two evils (Iran and Iraq) during the eight years of the war, Iraq was sent all matter of military hardware and intelligence by most of the countries now allied against Iraq despite the restrictions placed on such technology by the Coordinating Committee on Multilateral Export Controls (COCOM).[19] Almost two-thirds of all of these munitions came from the Soviet Union, China, and Eastern Europe. The following countries provided the following weapons to Iraq:

1.   The USSR--over 4,000 tanks and over 5,000 battlefield missiles

as well as hundreds of warplanes and armored vehicles, missile launchers, helicopters, anti-aircraft weapons, and artillery;

2. France--battlefield missiles, warplanes, radar and communications, nuclear technology, helicopters, anti-tank missiles, anti-ship missiles, armored vehicles, and anti-aircraft weapons;

3. Italy--biological and chemical technology, anti-ship missiles, and ship to air missiles;

4. China--tanks, warplanes, artillery, armored vehicles and anti-ship missiles;

5. Britain--training, radar and communications, helicopters, armored vehicles, and military construction;

6. The United States--training, nuclear technology, helicopters, and chemical and biological weapons technology;

7. West Germany--helicopters and chemical and biological weapons technology;

8. East Germany--tanks;

9. Poland--tanks, battlefield missiles, ammunition, and rifles;

10. Brazil--armored vehicles, battlefield missiles, and artillery;

11. Czechoslovakia--tanks and armored vehicles;

12. Chile--ammunition and rifles;

13. Jordan--warplanes and artillery;

14. Spain--helicopters and armored vehicles;

15. South Africa--artillery and ammunition;

16. Egypt--battlefield missiles and artillery;

17. Switzerland--armored vehicles;

18. Libya--armored vehicles;

19. Austria--artillery;

20. Romania--tanks;

21. Kuwait--tanks;

22. Canada--explosives, heavy equipment, steel and iron, industrial machines, computers, communications equipment, and parts for cars, trucks, and airplanes.[20]

The United States sold Iraq sensitive technology and made large numbers of loans to Iraqi companies. A U.S.-Iraq Business Forum was formed. Agricultural leaders were also interested in keeping American-Iraqi relations on a friendly level, since Iraq bought half of the American rice crop in 1989 and a significant proportion of American wheat. In all, $5 billion was earmarked for Iraq by the U.S. alone.

In spite of renewed international condemnation concerning the arming of potentially hostile foreign powers, the Gulf War created new opportunities for the arms merchants of the world. Often portrayed as an unsavory, hidden-in-back-rooms business, the arms trade is a multi-billion-dollar enterprise that has flourished for centuries. Even when the war with Iraq was nearly over, there began a mad scramble by most Mideastern countries to rearm or arm themselves. Once the war was over, many countries called for international arms embargoes. In a post-war news conference, President Bush said he hoped there would be less proliferation of all types of weapons, but, he added, "I don't think there will be any arms embargo."[21] After all, the United States has sold weapons for years and turned it into a very profitable business. One of the largest suppliers to Iraq was France. During the Iran-Iraq war, they sold Iraq defense systems and fighter planes. They considered Iraq such a good client that they let the *Mukhabarat* carry out assassinations in France and loaned aircraft and personnel to Iraq to use in the battles with Iran.[22] France also helped in the upgrading of the Scud missiles. In late 1989 and early 1990, France and Iraq had a disagreement over the amount owed by Iraq for work done. The French government, however, should have become suspicious when, in February 1990, Iraq put in an order for 900 million French francs' worth of advanced electronic equipment to a French company and paid for it in cash.[23]

West German companies were also involved in building up the Iraqi arsenal. These companies helped set up arms production facilities, and the Messerschmitt-Bolkow-Blohm Company was involved in the Iraqi missile development program.[24] Some Spanish companies provided Iraq with ammunition and bombs. Italian companies were an important supplier of naval equipment as well as aircraft. Norwegian enterprises provided explosives.

Swiss corporations provided aircraft and armored personnel carriers. The Austrian company Consultco designed the Saad-16 missile and developed a missile and chemical weapons research center.[25] Companies in such countries as Greece, India, North Korea, and South Africa and in the Eastern bloc and South American nations also provided arms.

Much has been said in media reports since the war began about a number of Western companies, located mainly, but not exclusively, in Germany, supplying different types of weaponry to Iraq. German and Austrian companies helped to build missiles and missile fuel research and production centers. In 1974, Mideastern technicians and Western compan-ies began to get involved in chemical research in Iraq. Companies in the Netherlands provided chemicals to Iraq, smuggling them through different agencies. They also helped with technicians training the Iraqis in the use of delivery systems.

One of the most infamous providers of arms for Iraq was the Chilean businessman Carlos Cardoen. He is one of the richest men in Chile, having made most of his fortune as a merchant of death. In 1988, Cardoen Industries did 95 percent of its business with Iraq. There were reports during 1990 that the Chilean government had already become increasingly embarrassed by reports of Cardoen's continuing commercial connections with Iraq, not least in view of the fact that Carlos Cardoen himself contributed $1 million to President Patricio Aylwin's election campaign and is an associate of the president's.[26] Cardoen even made use of intermedi-aries to sell more controversial goods to Iraq. It was reported in October 1990 that Libyan leader Muammar Qaddafi had acted as a intermediary between Iraq and Cardoen in exchange for a supply of fuel air explosive weapons.[27]

Iraq was thus portrayed by its leader and the Western media as the most powerful Arab country in the Middle East. There was no doubt about that. Its power, superlative for a Third World nation, was nevertheless still at the blueprint stage. Baghdad was not ready for a major war fought against countries on whom the Iraqi people were dependent. This was the greatest mistake of its leadership--which should have withdrawn from Kuwait while the going was good.

NOTES

1.   Miron Rezun, Post-Khomeini Iran and the New Gulf War (Que-bec: Centre québécois de relations internationales, 1991), pp. 13-14.

2.   This information was later collected by the London-based organ-ization, Amnesty International. This shows that Amnesty International does not always have valid data to work with when their sources are based on hearsay. The Iraqis did commit atrocities but they did not steal incubators,

and, if they did, they were not responsible for the murder of 300 infants. Our media liked to sensationalize this information, even if it meant distorting the truth.

3.   A doctor at the Mubarak al-Kabir Hospital in Kuwait said that there were hundreds of women awaiting abortions who had been gang-raped (*Time*, March 18, 1991).

4.   See Jean P. Sasson, *The Rape of Kuwait* (New York: Knights-bridge, 1991), p. 14.

5.   Abel Darwish and Gregory Alexander, *Unholy Babylon* (London: Victor Gollancz Ltd., 1991), p. 291.

6.   About 80 percent of Western European and Japanese oil comes from the Persian Gulf region.

7.   See Elizabeth Drew, "Letter from Washington," the *New Yorker*, February 4, 1991, pp. 174-187.

8.   Ibid.

9.   Ibid.

10.   Ibid.

11.   James A. Bill, *The Eagle and the Lion: The Tragedy of American-Iranian Relations* (New Haven: Yale University Press, 1988), p. 301.

12.   Myra MacPherson, *Long Time Passing: Vietnam and the Haunted Generation* (Scarborough: New American Library, 1984), p. 715.

13.   For some self-serving biographies of General Schwarzkopf, see the bibliography.

14.   Captain M. E. Morris, U.S.N. (Ret.), *H. Norman Schwarzkopf: Road to Triumph* (New York: St. Martin's Press, 1991), p. 38.

15.   Bob Woodward, *The Commanders* (New York: Simon and Schuster, 1991), p. 251.

16.   Ibid., p. 363.

17.   These included: military navigation, radar reconnaissance, photo reconnaissance, weather and communications, missile warning, and signal intelligence satellites.

18.   *Time*, March 4, 1991, pp. 36-37.

19.   COCOM is an organization set up by the United States and the other Western Allies after World War II to control sensitive technological exports.

20.   The foregoing information was taken from *Newsweek*, *Time*, and the *Sunday Star* (February 3, 1991, p. A12).

21.   *Manchester Guardian Weekly*, March 17, 1991, p. 9.

22.   Darwish and Alexander, *Unholy Babylon*, p. 139 and 141.

23.   Ibid., p. 143.

24.   Ibid., p. 146.

25.   Ibid., pp. 147-149.

26.   Ibid., p. 159.

27.   Ibid., p. 161.

6

The Storm

At the turn of the year, "Desert Shield" was transformed into "Desert Storm." The U.N. deadline had passed without any incident on January 15, 1991. James Baker and Tariq Aziz had met in Geneva but resolved nothing. Neither man was given authority by his superiors to make concessions to the other.[1]

Our gaze fixed on the television screen, we heard Bush declare on the 17th that the liberation of Kuwait had begun. In his heart of hearts, Bush had reasons to be elated. The Allied bombing of targets in Iraq and Kuwait was now official, beginning the day before at 2:32 A.M., Iraqi time. Saddam Hussein came on Baghdad Radio several times, exhorting his people and all Arabs to rise up against the cowardly infidels.

American military planning was prodigious. The wherewithal was awesome. The air war against Baghdad was conducted from a dingy Riyadh basement, dubbed "the Black Hole," by Lt. General Charles Horner[2] and Brig. General Buster C. Glosson. It was said that 99 percent of the targets were military. The first objective was to destroy Iraq's command and control network; second, to blind his radar and SAM anti-aircraft missiles while grounding his air force; third, to ravage Saddam's factories, depots, and labs; fourth, to completely destroy his airfields and ports, highways and bridges; and fifth, to inflict heavy losses among Saddam's elite troops dug in with artillery and tanks in underground bunkers along the Iraq-Kuwaiti frontier. Yet the Ba'ath party headquarters was also targeted, and so was the civilian telephone system. Iraqi military communications were, after all, also using the civilian lines. Baghdad's electricity was to be cut off, water tanks destroyed--and so, without willing it to happen, the Iraqi civilian population was made to feel the brunt of this high-tech war.[3]

It was folly and unrealistic for President Bush and the field commanders to declare that Iraqi civilian losses would be minimal or at least insignificant in comparison with other wars. This short war was going to last only six weeks. With the firepower the Americans had at their disposal it could not possibly have lasted longer. The Iraqi military--with the exception perhaps of the Republican Guard--was poorly fed, poorly led, and demoralized. Their tanks entrenched deep in the sands on the front lines could be picked off by laser-guided missiles and smart bombs. Baghdad, too, was very vulnerable, and the tens of thousands of innocent Iraqi soldiers who were about to die manning useless anti-aircraft batteries, Baghdad's children, the soon-to-be widowed wives, and their husbands--all of them, rallying, madly, to Saddam's call as if it were a holy crusade.

Before the Allied air armada began taking off from bases in Saudi Arabia or from aircraft carriers in the Gulf, the fate of the war in all its stages, from beginning to end, owed much to covert special operations. At the outset, Schwarzkopf was skeptical about using these special-operations forces. He regarded them as little better than "snake eaters" who had to be rescued by the regular army men when their harebrained schemes backfired.[4] Yet thanks to these brave men and their dangerous missions, the subsequent aerial bombardment of Iraq turned out to be nothing more than a turkey shoot, a Nintendo game.

Here is a highlight of some of their successful daredevilry.

a. Satellites and reconnaissance flights overflew Iraq as early as August 1990 looking for holes in the defenses.

b. Saddam's air defenses were caught napping the first night because of Colonel George Gray's strategy in using the U.S. Air Force's First Special Operations Wing to pierce Iraq's radar screen. A task force of both low-flying Pave Low helicopters and army Apache attack helicopters slipped across the Iraqi border, undetected, and punched a hole in Saddam's early warning screen. When Allied planes poured through the first night and bombed Baghdad's infrastructure and military installations, no planes were lost.

c. A psychological-operations team, using the largest non-nuclear bomb in the Pentagon's arsenal, produced an intelligence windfall that gave Schwarzkopf maps of the Kuwaiti minefields when Iraqi soldiers, frightened by the bomb, defected.

d. A team of six navy Seal commandos fooled the Iraqis into believing they were an amphibious invasion force of several thousand marines. Several Iraqi divisions were diverted east to repel the phony invasion--allowing Schwarzkopf's army to maneuver around to the west.

e. Army Special Forces teams slipped into Iraq before the ground war to act as human tripwires, warning Schwarzkopf's commanders every time Saddam's Republican Guard moved.

f. A top-secret team from Delta Force--America's elite counter-terrorist unit--played an instrumental role in tracking down and destroying Scud missiles aimed at Israel. On the last day of the war, Delta Force helped wipe out 26 Scuds that Saddam was preparing to launch at Israel in a last-ditch attempt to bring the Israelis into the war.[5]

THE WAR WAS WON IN THE AIR

Those crucial first days of the war also began with the launching of Tomahawk missiles from warships in the Persian Gulf and the Red Sea. Iraq tried to respond to the bombing in a number of different ways. They launched some planes to attack Saudi oil installations but only succeeded in damaging empty oil containers. Soon after this failure, it was reported that Iraqi planes were fleeing north and being safely sealed in bunkers. Others were spotted flying to Iran to seek a far safer haven. Iraq also launched Scud missile attacks on Israel and Saudi Arabia, which resulted in damage and injuries but no deaths directly attributable to the missiles. The American Patriot missile system was used, very successfully, to shoot down most of the incoming Scuds. After a week of the intense bombing, Iraq managed to display seven captured airmen (three Americans, one Italian, two Britons, and one Kuwaiti) on television and offered rewards of up to $30,000.00 for the capture of further airmen. Despite Saddam's assurances that the war was going well, a large number of Iraqi soldiers surrendered to Western troops and several Iraqi prisoners of war were taken from a U.S. raid on Kuwaiti oil platforms.

During the first full week of the war (January 21-27), the United States responded to the taking of Allied prisoners of war by accusing Iraq of abusing them for use in propaganda. They further insisted that Iraq let the International Red Cross examine the prisoners. Iraq replied that they would link the treatment of allied POWs with the Arab-Israeli dispute. They said that the Geneva Convention would be applied to them if the same provisions were applied to the people of Palestine. Iraq further announced that it had taken prisoners of war to economic and strategic targets throughout Iraq to act as human shields against Allied bombing.

On the battlefield, there was a small skirmish between Iraqi and Allied troops on the Kuwait-Saudi Arabian border at Khafjee. The Allies made the destruction of Scud missile launchers a top priority and deployed large numbers of aircraft to destroy them, using spy satellite and commando information. U.S. airmen flew as many as 3,000 to 4,000 sorties a day.

Iraq retaliated by waging an economic war. Iraqi solders set a number of oil wells and storage tanks on fire at the al-Wafra oil field in Kuwait and dumped oil into the Persian Gulf from the Sea Island Terminal in Kuwait. Bombing raids on Kuwait's oil-pumping facilities were successful in cutting off most of the oil that fed the massive slick.

Away from the front, another battle was raging: the war of foreign policy. In Europe, Germany admitted that it had delayed sending spare parts to Saudi Arabia and was, therefore, accused of hindering the war effort. Ironically, Germany then offered to send Patriot anti-missile batteries to Israel. Secretary of Defense Dick Cheney, in a news conference on January 22, announced that forcing Hussein out of Kuwait was no longer the final goal of the coalition. Destroying the Iraqis' military capability had become the new priority.

In the Middle East, Iraq began to trap refugees within its own territory by closing the Iraqi-Jordanian border. Palestinian demonstrators in Jordan marched in support of Iraq and asked to be armed to fight for their Arab brothers. King Hussein of Jordan, supporting the majority of Jordanians, wholeheartedly supported Iraq as the victim of aggression. As a result, in retaliation, Jordanians trying to enter Saudi Arabia, Syria, and Egypt were refused entry.

Trying to make political capital from this war, Iran suddenly came to the forefront of world attention. The Iranian leadership cautiously proposed a peace plan that called for an immediate ceasefire, and simultaneous withdrawal by both sides and, showing some empathy for the Iraqi cause, very slyly called for an immediate halt to Jewish settlements in the occupied West Bank. Teheran also called for Islamic forces to supervise the withdrawal of the coalition and Iraqi forces and supervise the lifting of the U.N. embargoes. But neither Saddam Hussein nor President Bush took the Iranians seriously. Iranian loyalty was always in question in the Persian Gulf.

The third week of the war (January 28-February 3) saw the continuation of Allied bombing with a priority set on Republican Guard positions and border defenses. Eleven Marines were killed by friendly fire in a struggle with Iraqi troops near the town of Umm Hujul. British, Saudi, and U.S. helicopters attacked more than a dozen small Iraqi boats. U.S. Marines took control of the tiny island of Umm al Maradim after the Iraqis fled from the advancing troops.

A total of 132 Iraqi planes sought sanctuary in Iran. Iran stated that it would keep the Iraqi planes within its borders. Estimated to be valued at $2.5 billion, the planes were expected to be used as partial payment for the $900 billion in reparations that Iran wanted from Iraq after the Iran-Iraq war.[6] Teheran in fact categorically refused a personal request from Saddam to return these planes. However, Iran's deputy parliamentary speaker warned that Iran would abandon its neutrality and fight alongside

Iraq if Israel joined in the war.

A Baghdad bomb shelter was destroyed by Allied bombing, resulting in the deaths of hundreds of civilians. The American military claimed that satellite information had shown the bomb shelter to be a military bunker and further claimed that Baghdad had put the civilians there deliberately knowing they would be killed. This whole argument echoed the American response to the downing of an Iranian civilian aircraft by the USS *Vincennes* during the Iran-Iraq war. A technical flaw in a British bomb caused it to drop off course from its intended target, a bridge, and it hit a crowded public market. At Saddam's direction, the Revolutionary Command Council of Iraq announced that it would withdraw from Kuwait under certain conditions, harking back to promises made before. But Bush refused to consider such things.

THE SOVIET PEACE PROPOSAL

Now it was the Soviet Union's turn to try to broker a peace between the belligerents. Gorbachev, Yeltsin, most of the other Russian leaders, the Ukrainians, and the Baltic states sided with the coalition. But the Soviet Muslims tended on the whole to sympathize with the cause of Saddam Hussein. Many Soviet Uzbeks and Azeris volunteered to go and fight for Baghdad. The Iraqi embassy was literally being inundated by letters of support from Central Asia and the Caucasus. Riots broke out in these areas, and the Moscow center became anxious to placate its southern rim. Controversy raged in the Soviet leadership.

It was interesting, though a bit strange, that Mikhail Gorbachev should appoint Yevgeny Primakov as his emissary to Baghdad.[7] Primakov was a knowledgeable diplomat and an academic with several books to his credit on the Middle East. But Primakov was a Jew, and, as such, unlikely to make an impact on Saddam Hussein. It was almost the same as sending U.S. Senator Metzenbaum to meet with Saddam, although it must be conceded the Russian Jew was intellectually superior to his American Jewish counterpart. Eventually, Primakov travelled to Baghdad three times and visited numerous Western leaders. While stressing that the USSR's interest in the Gulf War was different from Washington's, Primakov's position on the crisis underlined two things: "Hussein must be given a chance to save face, and he must be given guarantees if he agrees to withdraw from Kuwait."[8] The above-mentioned guarantees included one in which Iraq would not be attacked if it withdrew from Kuwait. The final peace plan presented by the USSR on February 21 agreed with Primakov's thinking on the matter.[9] It became apparent that Primakov was mediating between the United States and Iraq, rather than between Kuwait and Iraq. "Moscow's attempt to stand as a mediator between Iraq and the United States effectively makes the U.S.-led war effort seem as blameworthy as

Iraq's invasion of Kuwait."[10]

Iraqi foreign minister Tariq Aziz met with Mikhail Gorbachev and took Gorbachev's peace proposal to Baghdad. Washington's response to the initiative was simply that the Soviet peace plan fell far short of what was acceptable. Israel responded by stating that this plan would leave Saddam in power and Iraq's war potential intact, both of which were unacceptable. Iraq itself would not accept the proposal. Alas--the coalition rejected it out of hand and set its own condition: immediate and unconditional withdrawal from Kuwait. A few hours after this proposal was tabled, the Soviet Union announced a new proposal. But the coalition, in support of Bush himself, rejected this plan as well.

The air war against Iraq turned out to be an enormous success. One of the reasons for this triumph was the integration of the various air forces into a solid fighting force. Was this so unusual? After all, the American, British, French, Canadian, and Italian air forces had worked together before as part of the NATO. Further, the Saudi and other Gulf air forces had been trained by either the Americans or the British. All in all, the coalition flew over 110,000 missions with a loss of only 60 aircraft. On the other hand, the Iraqis lost 141 aircraft while 138 fled to Iran.[11]

The ground campaign, code-named "Desert Saber," began on February 24. On the very day it began, thousands of hungry, shell-shocked, and weary Iraqis gave up without a fight. In their escape from Kuwait, tens of thousands of Iraqi infantry and armor were strafed by Allied planes, blocking their avenues of escape to Iraq. In all 138 Allied soldiers were killed and 350 wounded, as compared to the last estimate I was able to obtain in early 1992 of one-quarter of a million Iraqis killed and 85-150,000 wounded. As to the results of the ground war, William J. Taylor, Jr., and James Blackwell concluded:

> In the final analysis, the Gulf war was the first ground war in history in which one side consistently and exclusively fought a strategy of attrition (Iraq) while the other side consistently and exclusively fought a strategy of movement (the coalition). The Iraqi military should have abandoned its strategy of attrition long before the ground campaign started; if it had, it might have avoided its virtual destruction.[12]

Saddam ordered his soldiers out of Kuwait on February 26--but he did not yet accept all U.N. resolutions. The Allies again rejected this and pressed on with the attack, hitting at Iraqi armor and men as they were retreating and continuing with the carpet bombing of Republican Guard positions along the Iraqi-Kuwait border. The only thing that actually slowed the Allied advance somewhat was the tattered and hungry Iraqi soldiers who begged to be allowed to surrender to the tank crews of the British

Desert Rats, to the U.S. Marines, even to the sundry Western journalists they were able to find. Thousands upon thousands surrendered. The war was over.

On February 28, at 12:00 A.M. EST, the United States and the coalition finally declared a ceasefire. Saddam and his Revolutionary Command Council had accepted all 12 U.N. resolutions (*see Appendix 1*), and a letter to that effect was promptly sent to the U.N. Security Council by Tariq Aziz. Meanwhile Iraq declared a victory and falsely stated that it had forced Bush to sue for peace. The Kuwaitis came out of hiding and immediately claimed that 22,000 Kuwaiti men had been abducted by Iraqi forces and 8,632 were being held as POWs.

Before I discuss the immediate aftermath of this war, let us briefly account for the role played during this crisis by other Arab and non-Arab countries.

GREAT BRITAIN

Arguably, the most dependable, if not the strongest, ally of the United States was Great Britain. Following the sudden resignation of Prime Minister Margaret Thatcher and the equally sudden ascension of her successor, John Major, the British sent a large number of troops and proved to be indispensable to the Allied cause. On January 15, the British parliament voted, by a margin of 534 to 57, to endorse the government's position of waging war against Iraq.

Many international observers were uncertain about the untried prime minister. John Major, the son of a trapeze artist, was voted the new Conservative prime minister after a career that included banking, membership in Parliament, and service as foreign secretary and as Chancellor of the Exchequer. Having replaced the Iron Lady, Major needed to prove himself. By standing solidly behind U.S. president George Bush, Major became one of the most popular British prime ministers in the last 30 years. What the Falklands factor once did for Margaret Thatcher the Gulf crisis did for John Major. The British proved themselves to be excellent fighters, being especially good at flanking maneuvers, and they played a large role in both the air and ground war. One potentially embarrassing result of British war coverage in Great Britain was the voting of Saddam Hussein as the BBC's "Man of the Year" by BBC World Service listeners. The *Sunday Times*, a London-based newspaper, criticized some of the young royals for not visiting British troops in order to boost morale, although they praised Prince Charles and Princess Diana for their efforts. During the last week of the war, Queen Elizabeth made her first wartime broadcast in which she hoped for a swift victory and peace and praised the country's armed forces.

FRANCE

The French were not as enthusiastic about the war as other Western countries, but they quickly accepted it and performed very well. Part of France's reluctance may be explained by its 4-million strong Arab population and its traditional colonial ties to the Maghreb, or North Africa. On January 29, Defense Minister Jean-Pierre Chevènement resigned from his cabinet post. He made no apologies for resisting a strong stand against Iraq. He was ridiculed in the press for being a co-founder of the Franco-Iraqi Friendship Association. The affair caused a considerable scandal in France.

Under General Michel Roquejoffre, the French took part in the air war with their few planes and included their Foreign Legion among their ground troops. They proved themselves to be especially adept at desert combat. After the war, Prime Minister François Mitterrand was expected to play a part in any Arab-Israeli talks, since Mitterrand has always endorsed the concept of a Palestinian state.

CANADA

Overshadowed by its more powerful Western allies, Canada nevertheless provided ships, planes, and personnel to the war effort. In early January, Prime Minister Brian Mulroney convened a war committee of cabinet ministers to study the role of Canada in the coalition. The Canadian parliament voted on January 22 to declare war on Iraq by a vote of 217 to 47. Public support at home ranged from wholehearted support to outrage at an apparent "puppeting" of Canada by the United States. Peace activists urged Ottawa to absolve itself by reassuming its traditional peacekeeping role.

Canadian embassies in the United States were swamped with calls from Americans who wanted to know if Canada would accept draft dodgers if the draft were instituted in the United States. Some Canadians who were working in the United States as permanent residents wanted to be sure they could still obtain a Canadian passport.

ITALY

Italy was reluctant to join in the war effort. It took many days of intense debate in the fractured Italian parliament for final assent to be granted, and the Italians participated in the air war.

GERMANY

Germany had been the source of much controversy since the war began. For example, West Germany was involved in the building of a steel-reinforced underground hideout under the Presidential Palace in Baghdad. When asked to comment, the chairman of the engineering firm said that, during the time, Hussein was seen as a Western ally for having fought Iran. On the whole, Germans were reluctant to support the war, but over 60 percent eventually considered it necessary once the air war began. Germany was very generous in helping Mideastern countries rebuild or recoup losses from the destruction. When the war ended, it was reported that German prosecutors charged 12 people with helping Iraq produce poison gas.[13]

BELGIUM

Belgium had been involved in the building of the underground bunkers and hangars where Hussein's air force was hidden. The Belgians also took part in the coalition.

THE EUROPEAN COMMUNITY AS A WHOLE

The European Community unequivocally gave aid to Mideastern countries that were adversely effected by the U.N. embargo. For example, it set aside $685 million for Jordan, Egypt, and Turkey. The European Community could only lose from the reluctance of some of its members to immediately respond to the crisis. As a result, these actions cast aspersions on the possibility of a united Europe. The actions of Germany were especially dismaying to the European Economic Community (EEC), since the Germans only reluctantly contributed to the war effort. In fact, Turkey accused Germany of acting in a cowardly way. Belgium was criticized for refusing to sell stocks of ammunition to Britain and allowing a visa to the spokesman of the Fatah Revolutionary Council.

JAPAN

The Japanese parliament failed to pass a vote to send armed forces to the Gulf in non-combat roles, although it did pass a resolution to send $9 billion in aid to the Allies. However, that resolution was unpopular; it could result in the defeat of the government in the next election. Japan also sent non-military Boeing 747s to Egypt to pick up Vietnamese refugees from Iraq. The Iraqi envoy in Tokyo then told the Japanese that they were considered an enemy of Iraq by announcing its aid package to the Allied forces. The Iraqi military specifically railed against the Japanese and vowed to shoot down any Japanese military aircraft sent to repatriate refugees. When the war ended, Japan announced that it would send a flotilla of navy minesweepers to help the multinational efforts to clear the

Persian Gulf of mines. This was the country's first military deployment abroad since World War II.

THE SOVIET UNION

The relationship that existed between the United States and the Soviet Union completely isolated Iraq. Moreover, not only did Gorbachev try to salvage a peace, but he adeptly used this opportunity to restore relations with Saudi Arabia and Bahrain. Gorbachev, with all his problems at home-- his political career was hanging by a thread--would not commit the Soviet army to participate in the war. His Soviet foreign minister, Eduard Shevárdnadze, stated that the Soviet Union would only intervene in the conflict if there was a direct threat to Soviet citizens in Iraq.

However, not everyone in the Soviet Union was pleased with Moscow's stance. Some commentators felt that if the Soviet Union became actively involved in the war it would lead to civil strife in the Muslim republics. In fact, many Soviet Muslims saw Hussein as a defender of the faith, much the same way as they saw the Ayatollah Khomeini.[14] Some Muslim leaders agitated against the United States and the coalition, and this led to demonstrations against Bush and Zionism in Moscow on January 19. The conservative paper *Sovetskaya Rossiya* accused the United States of genocide in Iraq while Major General Viktor Filatov, editor of the journal *Voennoistorichesky zhurnal* accused the United States of going beyond the U.N. mandate.[15]

Even the Supreme Soviets of the different Muslim republics could not agree on what position to take. The Supreme Soviet of Kirghizia wrote letters to the embassies of the Americans, the Kuwaitis, and the Saudis in Moscow asking them to cease hostilities, while Uzbekistan's Supreme Soviet appealed to Gorbachev to stop the conflict. The Supreme Soviet of Azerbaijan declared that the war went beyond the U.N. mandate and stated that the liberation of Kuwait was a pretext to protect U.S. oil interests.[16] The leader of a Russian nationalist fringe group--Pamyat--an anti-Zionist and anti-Semitic organization, praised Hussein for standing against Israel.

A military coup was brewing in the Soviet Union at this time. That would not happen until August, but, by February 13, a group of senior political officers from the KGB and the army openly condemned the Gulf War. Russian conservatives questioned Gorbachev's need to side with anti-Iraq forces. Gorbachev had indeed alienated some Communist party members because he was abandoning a 20-year ally in the Middle East. Gorbachev had to walk a fine line. As mentioned earlier, Gorbachev was navigating between Scylla and Charybdis: first, he had to please the Soviet military and Party, then he had to be sure not to anger the large Soviet Muslim population, and at the same time he had to show a conciliatory attitude to the West or else he would obtain no credits and investments to bail his country out of a precarious economic situation.

It is said that one area of potential humiliation for the Soviet military was the failure of the weapons the Russians gave the Iraqis.[17] Most Western military spokesmen, however, pointed out that Iraqi weapons were older models and that the Iraqis lacked the necessary training to use even these weapons properly. Further, Allied air supremacy was said to have been caused by their sheer numbers rather than through superiority of American over Soviet aircraft.[18] The Russians may not have a Stealth bomber capable of evading radar, but they have laser-guided bombs, heat-seeking missiles, and sea-launched cruise technology. They have night-fighting equipment and their helicopters and tanks are comparable to those of the United States--if not better. Nevertheless, it is quite clear that the Soviet military was nervous about the performance of Allied weapons in this war.

Two main schools of thought could be discerned in Soviet decision-making. The pro-West faction wanted to cooperate with the U.S.-led coalition. The Arabists, especially the Soviet armed forces, faction wanted the Soviet Union to continue its alliance with Iraq. What happened essentially was that for some time Gorbachev walked the fence between the two. Soviet foreign minister Eduard Shevardnadze pursued the pro-Western while the Jewish Arabist, Primakov, just as moderate, just as pro-Western, outlined a more nuanced, cautious line. Divisions were created between the Presidential Office and the Soviet Foreign Ministry. This was in a way similar to what occurred in the U.S. government before the outbreak of war. Primakov won out in this duel and was sent to Baghdad to strike a deal with Hussein. Irate and outmaneuvered, Shevardnadze resigned from his post, and his resignation cost Gorbachev a valuable ally. But the other Soviet Arabists of the military lost out altogether. So, they began plotting a coup to oust Gorbachev.

SAUDI ARABIA

The principal Arab ally in the coalition was, of course, Saudi Arabia. Not only was this country directly threatened by Hussein, but it was the United States' principal ally as well as the largest oil producer in the region. Realizing the problems of the post-war Gulf, the Saudis repeatedly stated that they were in favor of an international force in the region after the war. The war over, the Saudi government began to expel citizens of those countries that supported Iraq--Jordan, Yemen, Tunisia, Sudan, and Mauritania, not to mention most Palestinians.

KUWAIT

The exiled Kuwaiti government and Kuwaiti patriots were also a great help to the coalition. Thousands of Kuwaiti men returned to Kuwait in order to fight in the resistance after making sure that their families were safely placed in other countries. Kuwaitis also took part in the air and ground wars. But this country, with its 35 percent Palestinian population, faces a problem: after the war ended, Kuwaiti forces swept through Palestinian neighborhoods searching for collaborators. With their avowed support for Hussein, the Palestinians in Kuwait face discrimination and potential violence.

TURKEY

By mid-December of 1990, Turkey asked NATO to send several air units to guard its border with Iraq. Ankara received them in early January. Iraq threatened Turkey with unspecified "consequences" for allowing the coalition to stage a bombing attack against Iraq from Turkish soil. Turkey thus strengthened its own image in European eyes. Possibly because of this resolve during the crisis and its cooperation with the United States, Turkey believes--erroneously I think--that it is a better candidate now to join the EEC.

SYRIA

Syria came into a unique situation because of the war. Syria's leader, Hafez al-Assad, had been as associated with terrorism and repression as Saddam Hussein. He is part of the Alawite Muslim minority and is the leader of the country's Ba'ath party. He led the Ba'athist circle of air force officers that overthrew the existing regime in 1963 and brought the Ba'athist party to power. He went on to become commander of the air force and defense minister before becoming president in a bloodless coup in 1970.

The reported human rights abuses by the secret police and the government itself have been dreadful. Like Hussein, al-Assad had massacred over 20,000 of his own civilians, while trying to destroy the Muslim fundamentalist movement in 1982. The Muslim Brotherhood is a fundamentalist Sunni organization that has been against Westernization and secularization and, in 1980, demanded that al-Assad honor Syria's Human Rights Charter and hold free elections. On June 26, 1980, this Brotherhood tried to kill al-Assad. Crackdowns and murders followed. The Muslim Brotherhood fought back, and the massacre at Hama of February 1982 dwarfs the atrocities Saddam Hussein perpetrated against the Kurds. Syrian government troops, led by al-Assad's brother Rifaat, led a charge into Hama and, after many days' fighting, massacred thousands of people, mercilessly razing the town to the ground.[19] However, all this seems to have been forgotten and forgiven by George Bush and his White House advisors. The other Western nations followed in Bush's footsteps. Bush met with al-Assad in Geneva and embraced him as an ally. Britain restored diplomatic ties with Syria, and the European Community resumed economic aid. Syria received financial backing from the Kuwaiti and Saudi governments. Now Syria hopes that in return for its help in the war, which was absolutely insignificant, Israel will return the Golan Heights to it. Al-Assad even intimated to the Israelis that they could fly through his airspace on a retaliatory bombing mission against Iraq as long as they took a different route back.

To be sure, well before the outbreak of hostilities in the Gulf, Saddam Hussein asked the Syrians to join the Iraqi cause. Al-Assad refused. The two Ba'ath parties were nearly mortal enemies. Al-Assad did not wish to be outclassed. Besides, the enmity of the two went back to the Iran-Iraq war, when Syria supported Iran. Iraq supported Syria's main political opponent--the Maronite Christian general Michel Aoun in Lebanon.[20] There were other considerations that influenced Syria's thinking: the loss of the Soviet Union as its chief military patron, the return of Egypt to the Arab fold, the ending of an agreement under which Saudi Arabia and other Gulf states gave millions to Syria and Jordan for being the front-line states against Israel and the *Intifada* movement in Israel's Occupied Territories.

EGYPT

Egypt's debts to both Saudi Arabia and the United States were forgiven after they deployed 40,000 troops to Kuwait. Unlike other Arab countries, not all Egyptians supported Saddam Hussein.[21] The 1.5 million Egyptians who were employed in Iraq were ill-treated, given low wages, constantly harassed, and even murdered. Many Egyptians felt they had done enough for the Arab cause and suffered most during the Arab-Israeli wars. Egyptians were humiliatingly abandoned by all their Arab brethren after Cairo made peace with Israel in 1979. But secretly the Egyptian masses and the chronically poor supported Saddam Hussein against the Americans, for what it was worth. Like Soviet Central Asians, they felt this way primarily because they were Muslims.

IRAN

Iran has so far figured prominently in this narrative. Ostensibly neutral, this country had a significant impact on the Gulf War. On September 10, Iraq asked Iran to break the U.N. embargo and was refused. President Rafsanjani stood his ground and maintained his neutrality, although there was some opposition within his government. Ali Akbar Mohtashemi (the former interior minister), Mehdi Karrubi (speaker of the Iranian parliament), and Ahmad Khomeini (the late ayatollah's son) exhorted Iran to join Iraq in a "holy war" against America. Since the end of the war, Iran has stated that there will be no normal ties with the United States until Washington abandons its hostility toward Iran.

Perhaps the most interesting development between Iran and Iraq during this war was the flight of Iraqi warplanes to Iran. Some have conjectured that the sequestering of these planes was part of a secret deal. The transport planes, the French-built Mirages and Soviet-made MiGs--Saddam's best--were sent there in the same way that Iraq had sent the same planes for safekeeping to Jordan, Kuwait, Oman, Saudi Arabia, and North Yemen during the war against Iran. Moving the planes to Iran this time was not entirely unprecedented. This would mean that there was indeed a deal. I strongly suspect it was the work of Iraqi air force officers whose superiors had revolted against Saddam's rule and Saddam's wars. Some of these were probably Iraqi Shi'ites, others may have been disgusted when Saddam purged their commanders.[22]

Iran gained an immeasurable number of advantages since the war, all to Rafsanjani's credit. The European Community lifted its sanctions. Britain and Canada restored relations. Relations with the various Gulf emirates markedly improved, and the French announced that they would rebuild Iran's damaged Kharg Island oil terminal.

NOTES

1.   In mid-January, President Bush asked Congress for permission to use force against Iraq. On January 12, the Senate (by a vote of 52 to 47) and the House of Representatives (250 to 183) authorized Bush to take action.

2.   Horner was the coalition's supreme air commander.

3.   Shi'a shrines at Karbala and Najaf were not targeted. Neither was the giant statue of Saddam Hussein or the Al-Rashid Hotel, where all the foreign journalists were accommodated.

4.   *Newsweek*, June 17, 1991.

5.   For a more detailed report, see *Newsweek*, June 17, 1991.

6.   *Time*, April 8, 1991, p. 19.

7.   Yevgeny Primakov, Gorbachev's personal advisor, had travelled extensively throughout the Middle East in the 1960s and met Hussein many times as a correspondent for *Pravda*. He is currently finishing a book about his experiences during this war titled *The War Which Might Not Have Been*.

8.   Suzanne Crow, "Primakov and the Soviet Peace Initiative," *Report*

on the USSR--Radio Liberty, March 1, 1991, p. 16.

9. For the text of the Soviet peace plan, see Appendix 2.

10. Crow, "Primakov and the Soviet Peace Initiative," p. 17.

11. R. A. Mason, "The Air War in the Gulf," *Survival*, vol. 33, no. 3, May/June 1991, p. 225.

12. William J. Taylor, Jr., and James Blackwell, "The Ground War in the Gulf," *Survival*, vol. 33, no. 3, May/June 1991, p. 245.

13. See *Die Zeit*, March 12, 1991.

14. George Stein, "Soviet Muslims Divided on Gulf War," *Radio Liberty--Report on the USSR*, vol. 3, no. 8, February 22, 1991, p. 13.

15. Ibid., p. 14.

16. Ibid.

17. *Newsweek*, March 4, 1991, p. 44.

18. Stephen Foye, "The Gulf War and the Soviet Defense Debate," *Radio Liberty--Report on the USSR*, Vol. 3, no. 11, March 15, 1991, p. 1.

19. See Thomas L. Friedman, *From Beirut to Jerusalem* (New York: Anchor Books, 1989), p. 83.

20. Gideon Gera, "Iraq's Strategy--Towards Regional Dominance," *Middle East Focus*, vol. 13, no. 1, Spring 1991.

21. In fact, many Egyptians did not support either side. After the war, Egyptian Muslim fundamentalists hanged effigies of the leaders of both sides of the war.

22. See Miron Rezun, *Post-Khomeini Iran and the New Gulf War* (Quebec: Centre québécois de relations internationales, 1991).

Epilogue

When the tense Gulf episode finally ends, the careful student of Mideast affairs will reluctantly pore over the reasons why it started in the first place. Whatever the nature of the Iraqi state, whatever its internal ethnic and religious contradictions, Saddam Hussein emerged as the strongest, the most ruthless, and certainly the most stable leader since Iraq became independent. If this had not been the case, Egypt, Jordan, the Gulf sheikhdoms, indeed the majority of Arabs, would not have enlisted in his pan-Arab cause and his crusade against Iran. Much of the Western world also thought this way; otherwise Western countries would not have sold him the technical wherewithal he needed to preserve his own power and maintain stability in the Gulf.

During the American crusade against Saddam Hussein, the U.S. president constantly compared him with Adolf Hitler. He was demonized as the Butcher of Baghdad by Western leaders. George Bush repeatedly urged all Iraqis--Shi'ites, Kurds, and Sunnis alike--to overthrow this dictator who held the whole world hostage. Having punished Hussein for violating the sanctity of borders, the White House decided to give up on Iraq. Analysts ever since have justified this rationale for reasons of national interest. Except for Saddam's nuclear potential, which may or may not be a thing of the future, Israel has now been placated. Egypt, too, is satisfied. But Turkey hungrily covets rich Iraqi oil lands and is likewise content with the humbling of the Iraqi ruler. Kuwait has been promised (by Saddam, of course) compensation for damages done. Syria is hoping to lead the Arab world. The Palestinians, for their support of Iraq during the war, are in effect ostracized in the Gulf states. While this is going on, the U.S. secretary of state makes a desperate attempt at a peace conference on the Middle East to alleviate the plight of the Palestinians. The U.S. government hopes eventually to help with the formation of a Palestinian state. Of course, we are still a long way from such an eventuality. For such a thing to come about, the whole setting of the Middle East would have to undergo social and political change; the whole political reality and the psychology of its inhabitants would have to be altered. In the meantime, Israel is still being threatened.

The United States did not lead a coalition to the Gulf just to oust Saddam Hussein from Kuwait. It did not get involved just to keep the oil flowing. Nor was it to protect the pro-American Arab states, nor Israel, for that matter. Perhaps it was because Saddam was close to achieving a deliverable nuclear weapon? Perhaps it was for all the reasons above?

The war over, who is to say whether Saddam really expected to stay in Kuwait? It is clear that George Bush and the American military derogated all of Iraq's conciliatory gestures. Did not U.S. forces and the U.S. command overcommit themselves to a course of action? Did not the American administration pay lip service to others' efforts at finding some diplomatic solution? How strange, too, that King Hussein of Jordan, who turned his back on the Americans during the war, was forgiven by them as if nothing untoward happened when the crisis ended.

Stranger still is the way a huckstering General Schwarzkopf was packaged by the media as a war hero for the American public. The general was hardly a war hero. He never risked his life. The whole war waged against Saddam Hussein by the United States was a risk-free exercise. As one guilt-ridden British journalist mockingly put it:

> Schwarzkopf sat bunkered in a fortified command center far from any bullets. No enemy planes were in the skies. No enemy ground troops, just poorly armed Iraqi conscripts who gave up after 100 hours of hapless combat . . . he oversaw an air war that one of his pilots called "a turkey shoot" after blowing away defeated, unarmed Iraqis on the roads north. How about having him make a speech on the topic of swords into stockshares, now that U.S. arms sales to Gulf nations have resumed in preparation for the next war and next U.S. intervention?[1]

But the tempest had not yet been spent. A hideous aftermath immediately followed. Saddam Hussein callously carried the war to his own people. The United States could but this time was not going to intervene.

THE TRAGEDY OF THE IRAQI SHI'ITES AND KURDS

The saturation bombing of Iraq knocked out electrical plants and water tanks, roads and bridges. All Iraqis began to suffer from epidemics of typhus and other diseases, worsened by malnutrition. The hospitals lacked antibiotics and equipment to help sick adults and starving infants. Despair was sweeping the entire country. The people revolted against Saddam Hussein just as President Bush had encouraged them to do.

Fighting between Saddam's forces and pro-Iranian Shi'a fundamentalists soon began to gain control of southern Iraq. The port city of Basra and the city of Nasiriyah quickly fell to the Shi'ites. The next day, the Republican Guard recaptured Basra while the Shi'ites claimed control of Karbala and Najaf. On March 10, the Republican Guard stormed Karbala and killed 500 rebels. Thousands of Shi'ites fled to Iran.

In northern Iraq, the Kurds rose to make a last-ditch effort to gain independence and seized control of the cities of Sulaymaniyah and Kirkuk. Demonstrators in Mosul stormed two prisons and released 4,000 prisoners. The Iraqi central authorities responded by rounding up 5,000 Kurds, mostly women and children, and used them as human shields to avert an attack on the city of Kirkuk. On the 15th of March 1991, rebels took control of the main border crossing between Turkey and Iraq and said that they were in control of 95 percent of Kurdistan.

These people were responding to Bush's call for the overthrow of Saddam. But who was to replace him? Most of the opposition leaders were either dead or in exile. Saddam was very careful to make sure that he was the only option for the governing of Iraq. If Saddam disappeared, Iraq would be unstable, hard to govern, anarchic.

Britain had already made contacts with the London representatives of the two major Iraqi opposition parties. Syria and Iran likewise started organizing Iraqi opposition groups in the hope of influencing events in a post-war Iraq. On March 13, in Beirut, 23 Iraqi opposition factions decided to coordinate their anti-Hussein strategy and pledged to set up a transitional coalition government to lead Iraq to democracy if and when Saddam was toppled. But most of these opposition groups were made up of Kurds who had a particular agenda. For one thing, they would demand their own country. Worse, they could and already did stir up separatist fires among the Kurdish minorities in Turkey, the Soviet Union, and Iran. Syria would in the end demand land from Iraq, and so would Iran.

Turkey has long coveted Iraq's oil-rich Mosul Province. The Shi'a majority of Iraq wanted to form a separate country, or join Iran. A *Time* article ruminated about the quandary in these words: "The Lebanonization of Iraq would become part of the unhappy legacy of foreign involvement in the Middle East, a result the West is anxious to avoid."[2] A completely prostate and dismembered Iraq would create a political vacuum in this area, a vacuum that all of these states would seek to fill, with the possibility of renewed hostilities.

NO SOLUTION IN SIGHT

If the country were to be fragmented into three separate individual parts, the problem with any coalition is that of its leadership. The Kurds could not accept an Islamic Shi'a leadership. One of their leaders, Jalal Talabani, once said that "an Islamic state in Iraq is intolerable."[3] Speculation on the type of leadership that would grow out of a winning rebellion seemed rather vain given the brutal crackdown by the Hussein regime on these rebellions. Still, given the fact that Kurds make up 21 percent of the Iraqi population and the Shi'ites make up 53 percent, it would seem that these segments of the population must be represented.

The Shi'a rebellion in the south was disorganized and never really stood a chance of succeeding. U.S. policy advisors were suspicious of the Shi'a south. One of its groups, the al-Daawa, was involved in suicide bombings of U.S. embassies, airline hijackings, and assassination attempts in the Gulf states.

When Saddam turned his attention to the south, the Shi'ites had very little chance of organizing themselves. They failed to form a command and communications system and were dependent upon weapons and ammunition left behind by retreating Iraqi soldiers.[4] American soldiers in the occupied Iraqi zone were forced to watch helplessly as these civilians were killed and their towns destroyed. They extended as much medical and humanitarian aid as they could to the survivors who stumbled into their territory.

As for the Kurds, they had long been promised their own independent state. When the French and British carved up the Ottoman Empire, they signed the Treaty of Sèvres with Kurdish leaders in 1920. This treaty promised the Kurds and the Armenians their own state. Turkish nationalists under Kemel Ataturk refused to accept the treaty, and the 1923 Treaty of Lausanne recovered both areas for Turkey. Their promises broken, the British eventually annexed Kurdistan to Iraq.

It seemed unlikely that the Americans would want to become involved in a civil war in Iraq. The attitude that prevailed in Washington circles was best summed up in a remark made by a State Department official: "It probably sounds callous but we did the best thing not to get near [the Kurdish revolt]. They're nice people, and they're cute, but they're really just bandits. They spend as much time fighting each other as they do fighting the central authority. They're losers."[5]

Flushed with success for their routing of Saddam's army, some U.S. policy analysts realized the hypocrisy of leaving the Kurds under Saddam's brutal heel. They saw it as the abandoning of an ally and a compliance with genocide. One U.S. official stated, "It seems to me just like Hungary in 1956. Having called on people to overthrow their repressive leadership, we just sit back and watch them get slaughtered." Other commentators offered a different analogy: "the Red Army halting outside Warsaw in 1944 and doing nothing to stop a Nazi massacre of the Jewish ghetto residents who had risen in revolt."[6] The New York Times conservative columnist

William Safire charged that Bush was becoming "the third U.S. president to sell out the Kurds. Richard Nixon did it in the '70s, at the behest of the Shah of Iran for regional stability; Ronald Reagan did it in 1988, by rewarding Saddam Hussein with greater commodity credits despite the poison-gassing of Kurds in Halabja."[7]

Perhaps General Schwarzkopf had some remorse. In an interview, he stated he had wanted to continue the war and remove Hussein from power; but the U.S. president forced him to stop. Later, apparently at the risk of presidential censure, he recanted this statement.

It was obvious that President Bush felt Saddam would defeat the rebellion with the help of the leaders of the armed forces and the Ba'ath party. Bush was also apprehensive that the rebellions could dismember the country. The Allies feared this the most of all. Turkey, Syria, and Iran did not want the Kurds to have their own country; it could have led to their own Kurdish minorities rising in rebellion.

Furthermore, Bush declared he had no mandate to go into Iraq to interfere in a civil war. He argued that the U.N. resolutions contained nothing about protecting the Kurds and Shi'ites from Saddam. What was forgotten, incidentally, was how Bush had sent troops to the Gulf before the United Nations had passed any resolutions against the Iraqi invasion of Kuwait.

When Saddam's forces began to overrun the rebels in the north, the Kurds, knowing what Saddam was capable of, fled to the north and to the east to get away from his forces. In cars, buses, tractors, and on foot, the Kurds carried themselves and their meager possessions across the wind-swept, icy mountain wastes on their way to a freedom that lay nowhere. Without food, clean water, and warm clothes for the arduous journey, the old, the infirm, women, and infants died from malnutrition and cold. Pictures of the squalid camps where the refugees were forced to live were shown across the world. In the make-shift camps of shredded plastic that doubled as tents there was no sanitation. Human waste ran down the hills into the small streams, polluting the environment and causing cholera to spread.

Over two million Kurds converged on the borders of Turkey and Iran to flee the attacking Iraqi troops. For a while the world watched and ignored. Having shot down two Iraqi planes for bombing the frantic Kurds, U.S. forces stood by and did nothing as Saddam's helicopters dropped napalm and incendiary bombs on the Kurdish villages.

Only Iran let both Kurds and Shi'ites into the country. Iran's generosity toward them is hardly based on altruism. It is designed partly to mollify Iran's own restless Kurdish minority, which makes up 9 percent to 12 percent of the population, and partly to improve the country's deplorable human-rights image. The Iranians are also desperately seeking to improve their international reputation and to reassert their role as the only major power in the region.

Iran now walks a fine line. Besides facing irredentism from their own Kurds, Iran already has more than three million Afghan refugees, not to mention 250,000 Iraqi Kurds from before this exodus. To add to Iran's problems, on April 14, Bahaa Din Ahmad, a senior Ba'athist party member in Iraq, charged that the Iranians had started the rebellion in the north and south. On the 15th, Iran retaliated by accusing Iraq of sending troops across the border and of occupying Iranian territory three kilometers from the border. Teheran radio reported that Iraqi troops attacked fleeing Kurds at the Iranian border.

The Turkish government, on the other hand, has discriminated against its own Kurdish minority by not counting them as Kurds. They are noted on census reports as "mountain Turks," and until recently Ankara considered it a crime for a Kurd to speak the Kurdish language. Some of the Turkish military even suspected that Saddam was deliberately sending the Kurds across the border in order to take revenge on Turkey for backing the coalition against his government.[8]

Across Europe and the United States, debates and controversies raged over the Kurdish question. On April 3, the newly retired Iron Lady, Margaret Thatcher, gave everyone the hint the world was waiting for. "The Kurds," she said, "don't need talk, they need practical action. It should not be beyond the wit of man to get planes there with tents, food and warm blankets. It is not a question of standing on legal niceties. We should go now."[9]

Like other presidents before him, George Bush listened to Thatcher's advice. On April 5, Bush called for supplies to be sent to the area by American marines and Special Forces in an operation called "Operation Provide Comfort." It was the noblest undertaking in the whole war, worthy now of the United States as the only remaining superpower.

The U.N. Security Council passed Resolution 678, in which the Allies were authorized to act to bring peace and security to the region, and Resolution 688 condemned Iraq's repression of its own people and called on Secretary-General Perez de Cuellar to help the Kurdish refugees. The United Nations sent its own delegates to Baghdad to negotiate with Hussein. The European Community pledged $180 million in humanitarian aid to the camps. Israel, too, began a number of airdrops of supplies, which the Iraqi government said infringed on their sovereignty. In the meantime, the U.S. government ordered its armed forces to feed, shelter, and clothe 700,000 Kurdish refugees for 30 days in northern Iraq--it was the largest relief program mounted in modern military history.

We must be mindful of the fact that the Kurds form the fourth largest national group in the Middle East, after the Arabs, Iranians, and Turks. Moreover, they were established in the Taurus and Zagros mountains long before any of the aforementioned three. In a Middle East so artificially demarcated, they deserve a state no less than the Palestinians. Amid the sympathy and goodwill shown to these people as a result of their suffering, there are still voices in the United States who do not condone America's humanitarian policies.

One of these critics is a journalist turned academic, Stephen C. Pelletiere, a proven hack (among other "experts" in Washington), warning the U.S. military that supporting the Kurds and their "*agas,*" or feudal lords, is a lost cause. He appeals to us with passionate words: "Within the Middle East the Kurds have the reputation of being desperate characters, inveterate disturbers of the peace, and not at all reliable to deal with."[10] But who, may one ask, is reliable enough to deal with in the Middle East?

The United States has officially declared that it is dedicated to the overthrow of Saddam Hussein. But the opportunity to oust the Iraqi dictator was lost when the Americans withdrew their forces after the war; it was also lost when the United States failed to support the Kurdish rebellion with arms and military assistance. At this time of writing, Washington is awash with rumors of helping Iraq's minority of 3.5 million Kurds, to launch a final assault against Saddam Hussein in Baghdad. This question is mooted. Some Iraqi opposition figures contend that helping the Kurds is not the way. They want Washington to ground Iraq's helicopter fleet and provide inducements for the Iraqi soldiers to defect in large numbers into Kurdistan. There a provisional army and government could be built to march back to Baghdad and destroy Saddam's regime.

Another harebrained scheme, this time coming from Saudi Arabia, suggests the United States and Saudi Arabia provide covert financing for small anti-armor missiles so that the Kurds could better defend themselves against Iraqi helicopter gunships and tanks. The situation remains at an impasse. But for how long?

As Saddam Hussein tightens his inner circle of government with relatives and Takriti supporters, the noose around him also tightens. He will surely not die at the hands of the Americans (or am I just being naive?). The Iraqi dictator has other, far more ruthless, enemies. We will watch and see, as the plot thickens and thickens.

NOTES

1. Colman McCarthy, "Spoils for the Victor," *Manchester Guardian Weekly,* July 14, 1991, p. 19.

2. *Time,* March 18, 1991, p. 26.

3. *Manchester Guardian Weekly,* March 17, 1991, p. 8.

4. *Time,* April 15, 1991, p. 18.

5. *Newsweek,* April 15, 1991, p. 27.

6. *Time,* April 8, 1991, p. 17.

7.   *Newsweek*, April 8, 1991, p. 19.

8.   The Turks have thus not let many Kurds in, for fear that they would join with Kurdish Turks to form a political bloc.

9.   See *Time*, April 15, 1991.

10. See Stephen C. Pelletiere, *The Kurds and their Agas: An Assessment of the Situation in Northern Iraq* (Carlisle Barracks, Penn.: Strategic Studies Institute, U.S. Army War College, 1991), p. 1.

Appendix 1

U.N. Resolutions Adopted Against Iraq During the War

1. Resolution 660--condemned the invasion of Kuwait and demanded that Iraq withdraw its forces--adopted August 2, 1990

2. Resolution 661--imposed sanctions on trade to Iraq except for food and medicine--adopted August 6, 1990

3. Resolution 662--declared Iraq's annexation of Kuwait null and void--adopted August 9, 1990

4. Resolution 664--demanded Iraq allow foreign nationals to leave the country and cancelled its order to close diplomatic missions--adopted August 18, 1990

5. Resolution 665--permitted states to use limited naval force to ensure compliance with economic sanctions--adopted August 25, 1990

6. Resolution 666--approved food shipments to Iraq and Kuwait for humanitarian purposes only if distributed by approved international groups--adopted September 13, 1990

7. Resolution 667--condemned raids by Iraqi troops on diplomatic missions in Kuwait--adopted September 16, 1990

8. Resolution 669--adopted a measure that entrusted its sanctions committee with evaluating requests for assistance from countries suffering because of the trade embargo--adopted September 24, 1990

9.   Resolution 670--prohibited air traffic with Iraq and Kuwait except for humanitarian reasons--adopted September 25, 1990

10. Resolution 674--asked states to document financial loss and human rights violations resulting from the invasion adopted October 29, 1990

11. Resolution 677--asked the U.N. secretary-general to safeguard a smuggled copy of Kuwait's pre-invasion population register--adopted November 28, 1990

12. Resolution 678--authorized all states to use force against Iraq unless it withdrew from Kuwait on or before January 15--adopted November 29, 1990

In this last case, China abstained. In nearly every other instance, Cuba and Yemen either opposed or abstained from voting on resolutions.

Appendix 2

Peace Proposals

INITIAL IRAQI PEACE OFFER

1. Complete halt in hostilities;

2. Abandonment of other 11 U.N. resolutions;

3. An end to the economic embargo and sanctions;

4. Pullout of coalition forces and removal of new weapons in Israel;

5. Israel's withdrawal from the West Bank, the Golan Heights, and the southern part of Lebanon;

6. An insistence that the U.N. Security Council apply the same measures used against Iraq to Israel;

7. The recognition of Iraq's historic rights;

8. Use of democracy to create a new government in Kuwait;

9. Rebuilding of Iraq by the coalition;

10. Cancellation of Iraqi debts;

11. Subsidization of poor Persian Gulf countries by wealthy ones;

12. Provisions for Gulf countries to decide on security measures within the region;

13. An end to all foreign military bases in the Gulf.

THE FIRST SOVIET PEACE PROPOSAL

1. The unconditional withdrawal (within a fixed period) of Iraq from Kuwait beginning 24 hours after a ceasefire;

2. The promise of no punishment for Saddam Hussein and the dropping of sanctions when the withdrawal was two-thirds complete;

3. All U.N. resolutions to be cancelled when withdrawal ends;

4. All POWs to be immediately released;

5. The promise that the Soviet Union will secure the structures and borders of Iraq;

6. The Palestinian problem, and other Mideastern problems, to be debated.

COALITION RESPONSE TO SOVIET OFFER

1. Iraq must begin withdrawing from Iraq by noon EST on February 23;

2. This withdrawal must be completed within a week;

3. Within 48 hours, Iraq must remove troops from Kuwait City and allow the return of the government of Kuwait;

4. Iraq must withdraw from the Saudi-Kuwait and Saudi-Iraq borders and from Bubiyan and Warbah islands and from the Rumaila oil fields;

5. In accordance with United Nations Security Council Resolution 660, Iraq must withdraw to their positions of August 1 within one week;

6. Iraq must release all POWs and civilians with bodies of dead servicemen in cooperation with the International Red Cross within 48 hours of the beginning of a withdrawal;

7. Iraq must remove all explosives and booby traps and designate military liaison officers to work with Kuwaiti and other forces on the withdrawal's operational details;

8. Iraq must cease all combat flights over Iraq and Kuwait except to transport troops to Iraq;

9. Iraq must cease all destructive actions against Kuwaiti citizens and property and release all Kuwaiti detainees;

10. The United States and coalition will not attack retreating Iraqi forces;

11. Any breach of these terms would bring an "instant and sharp" response from coalition forces.

SOVIET COUNTER-PROPOSAL

1. Implementation of U.N. Resolution 660;

2. Withdrawal beginning one day after the ceasefire and being completed within 21 days (with a pullout of Kuwait City within 4 days);

3. All U. N. Security Council resolutions would be null and void after completion of the withdrawal;

4. All POWs would be released within 72 hours after the ceasefire;

5. Supervision of the withdrawal would be conducted by a peace-keeping force determined by the Security Council.

Appendix 3

Iraq's Nuclear Program

1959--Iraq establishes an interest in nuclear energy when it establishes the Iraqi Nuclear Energy Committee and joins the International Atomic Energy Agency (IAEA).

1969--Iraq signs the Nuclear Non-Proliferation Treaty.

1972--Iraq ratifies the Nuclear Non-Proliferation Treaty.

1978--The Mossad becomes concerned over Iraqi nuclear research and establishes "Operation Sphinx" to penetrate the Iraqi nuclear effort and to obtain information on the French-built Osirak project.

June 8, 1981--Israel attacks and completely destroys the Osirak nuclear plant in Iraq.

July 1990--Rumors circulate in intelligence circles (chiefly in the Mossad and the CIA) that Iraq has developed an initiator that can be used to detonate a nuclear device. Iraq is also rumored to have adequate plutonium and uranium for its nuclear program.

April 3, 1991--The U.N. Security Council passes a resolution to strip Iraq of all missiles and chemical, biological, and nuclear weapons.

April 26--The IAEA gives Iraq until April 26 to list the locations of weapons-grade nuclear material after Iraq informs it that it has no nuclear weapons.

June 13--An Iraqi defector (a scientist) tells interrogators that Iraq was using 1940s technology to make weapons-grade uranium in a nuclear project previously undetected by the United States. The scientist states that more than 36 kilograms of enriched uranium had been produced at the Saad 16 site near Mosul.

June 22--Inspectors tour the Al Gharaid site and note that machinery was removed.

June 26--The United States accuses Iraq of carrying out a secret nuclear weapons program and demands it open all installations to internal inspection. During an earlier visit to research sites at Tuwaitha and Tarmiya in May, the IAEA sealed 39 kilograms of uranium that Iraq had declared.

June 27--President Jean-Jacques Bechio (from the Ivory Coast) of the U.N. Security Council asks Iraq to make available the equipment used to enrich uranium removed from an army base to avoid detection by U.N. inspectors. Representatives of France, Belgium, Austria, Britain, Ecuador, and Romania demanded that Baghdad cooperate with U.N. inspection teams.

June 28--Hussein orders officials to cooperate fully with U.N. team. U.N. inspectors had previously said that they were barred from two nuclear sites and soldiers had fired in the air to try to stop them from taking photographs. The U.N. team had also asked to visit one suspected nuclear site at the Abu Gharaib military complex and had been made to wait three days. At an inspection at a site near Al Fallujah, the inspectors saw what may have been the equipment taken from Al Gharaid. Iraqi soldiers tried to sneak the machinery out. The inspectors followed the convoy and filmed it. They were shot at.

June 31--Three U.N. troubleshooters (Rolf Ekeus, head of the U.N. Special Committee set up to scrap Iraq's weapons of mass destruction, Hans Blix, head of the IAEA, and Yasushi Akashi, U.N. Under-Secretary General) arrive in Iraq and deliver a Security Council demand that Iraq hand over equipment suspected of being part of a secret nuclear weapons program.

July 3--A mission from U.N. Security Council wraps up three days of talks without securing inspection of equipment that experts say could be used to make nuclear bombs. The first Iraqi ballistic missiles are destroyed by Iraqi soldiers supervised by U. N. officials. The United Nations pulls out its nuclear inspectors.

July 7--A 37-member U.N. team visits two nuclear sites in a study to determine the response of U.S. led coalition to charges that Iraq is cheating on nuclear-site disclosure.

July 8--Iraq acknowledges that it had a secret program to enrich uranium.

July 9--A 24-member U.N. team arrives to oversee the destruction of Iraq's non-conventional weapons under the Persian Gulf War cease-fire agreement.

July 11--Saddam's new wave of purges results in the deaths of high-ranking Shi'ite army officers. Among those killed are Major-General Yalchin Omar, hero of the Iran-Iraq war.

July 12--President George Bush approves a target list of Iraqi military command and control centers to be bombed if Baghdad does not destroy its nuclear technology.

July 14--France and the United States say they will renew military force if Iraq fails to disclose and eliminate its nuclear-weapons capability.

July 15--Iraq says it is taking steps to defend itself against a possible U. S. strike on military and nuclear sites. Britain joins France and the United States in saying that it would use force to stop Iraq from acquiring nuclear weapons.

July 16--Iraq invites the Arab League to send inspectors.

July 17--The head of the U.N. inspection team, Dimitri Perricos, says Baghdad seems to have come clean on its nuclear secrets. Inspectors investigate two uranium enrichment plants that were undeclared. The team accounted for all the calutrons (electromagnetic isotope separation equipment of World War II vintage) in Iraq's nuclear program. Iraq had developed and built them themselves.

August 15--The United Nations passes Resolution 707, which gives the U.N. inspectors the right to inspect suspected Iraqi weapons sites unannounced.

Week of September 14--U.N. inspectors fly home saying that they had been prevented from using their helicopters to swoop down unannounced on suspected Iraqi weapons sites.

September 18--Hussein offers to make these helicopter flights legal if Iraqis could be on board each flight, no aerial photographs are to be taken, and certain parts of Baghdad are declared off-limits. The Americans refuse and threaten military action. American fighter aircraft are put on alert.

September 23--Iraqis detain a U.N. team that has taken three car-loads of documents from an atomic-energy office. The Iraqis detain the team and make them give up most of the information. Using a copier and fax machine, the team transmits most of it to the IAEA. Interestingly enough, on entering the office, the inspectors find filing cabinets marked "remove before U. N. inspection."

September 24--The Iraqi foreign minister and U.N. ambassador deli-ver a letter to the Security Council letting the inspection teams fly where they wished. However, the same day, the Iraqis surround a bus holding the inspectors who had just found a cache of documents on Iraq's nuclear program. The inspectors are told they cannot leave until they turn over the documents. Bush orders his defense chiefs to send 50 aircraft to Saudi Arabia and dispatches 96 Patriot missiles to Saudi Arabia as well.

September 26--The Iraqis let the inspectors go provided they sign an inventory of all documents taken by them.

Week of October 5--U.N. inspectors conclude that Iraq has been try-ing to build hydrogen as well as nuclear bombs. So far, they have discovered 16 missile sites that the Iraqis failed to declare. Because of the U. N. inspectors' perceived failure to adequately discover all evidence of nuclear material, on October 4, Israel sends warplanes over Iraq's western desert to search for more nuclear evidence. Needless to say, the Iraqis are extremely upset.

October 11--Another U.N. inspection team arrives in Iraq to search for any weapons sites near the town of Mosul. The United Nations passes a resolution extending indefinitely its inspection regime.

March 11, 1992--The U.N. Security Council made one of its harshest criticisms of Iraqi President Saddam Hussein since he invaded Kuwait on August 2, 1990. Iraqi deputy prime minister Tariq Aziz was pres-ented a series of complaints about Iraq's failure to disclose and destroy all of its ballistic missiles as well as nuclear, chemical, and biological weapons programs. It was suggested that if Saddam did not comply with Persian Gulf war resolutions, force might be used again.

Select Bibliography

Al-Hamad, Torky. "*Al-Hadaf wal-injazat fi Tajribat Majlis al-Taawun al-Kha-liji: al-Manzour as-Siyasi*" [The Goal and the Accomplishment in the Gulf Cooperation Council Experiment: The Political View]. Paper presented to the Conference on Development, Bahrain, January 3-5, 1990.

Al-Hamad, Torky. "*Al-Ideologiyya wat-Tanmeyya fil-Khaleej: Ba'hth fil-Thaqafa al-Ijtima'iyya*" [Ideology and Development in the Gulf: A Study in Social Culture]. Unpublished paper, Department of Political Science, King Saud University, Riyadh, Saudi Arabia, 1989.

Al-Jallal, Abdul Aziz. "*Majlis al-Ta'awun li-Dowal al-Khaleej al-'Arabiyya-al-'Ahdaaf wal-Injazaat: Taqweem al-Masseerah*" [Co-operation Council for the Arab Gulf States--Goals and Accomplishments: An Assessment]. A commentary on the paper presented by Dr. Torky Al-Hamad at the Conference on Development, Bahrain, January 3-5, 1990.

al-Khalil, Samir. *Republic of Fear: The Politics of Modern Iraq.* Berkeley: University of California Press, 1989.

Al-Neibari, Abdullah Mohammed. "*Taqyeem Tajrubat Majlis al-Taawun li-Dowal al-Khaleej al-'Arabiyya*" [Evaluation of the Cooperation Council for the Arab Gulf States Experiment] A rejoinder at the Conference on Development, Bahrain, January 3-5, 1990.

Axelgard, Frederick W. *A New Iraq?--The Gulf War and Implications for U.S. Policy.* New York: Praeger, 1988.

Ayoub, Mahmoud M. *Islam and the Third Universal Theory: The Religious Thought of Mu'-ammar al-Qadhdhafi*. London: KPI, 1987.

Aziz, Tariq. *Iran-Iraq Conflict: Questions and Discussions*. Trans. Naji Al-Hadithi. London: Third World Center for Research and Publishing, 1981.

Barash, David. *Introduction to Peace Studies*. Belmont, Cal.: Wadsworth, 1991.

Bill, James A. *The Eagle and the Lion: The Tragedy of American-Iranian Relations*. New Haven: Yale University Press, 1988.

Bulloch, John. "A Talent for Terror," *Montreal Gazette*, January 26, 1991.

Bulloch, John and Henry Morris. *The Gulf War: Its Origins, History, and Consequences*. London: Methuen, 1989.

Cardri (Committee Against Repression and for Democratic Rights in Iraq). *Saddam's Iraq: Revolution or Reaction?* London: Zed Books, 1989.

Childs, Nick. *The Gulf War*. East Sussex, England: Wayland, 1989.

Chubin, Shahram and Charles Tripp. *Iran and Iraq at War*. Boulder, CO: Westview, 1988.

Cohen, Roger and Claudio Gatti. *In the Eye of the Storm: The Life of General H. Norman Schwarzkopf*. New York: Farrar, Straus and Giroux, 1991.

"Constitution of the Arab Resurrection Socialist Party, The," Sami A. Hanna and George H. Gardner, eds., *Arab Socialism--A Documentary Survey*. Leiden, Netherlands: E. J. Brill, 1969.

Cordesman, Anthony H. *The Gulf and the West: Strategic Relations and Military Realities*. Boulder, CO: Westview, 1988.

Crusoe, Jonathan. "Economic Outlook: Guns and Butter, Phase Two?," in Frederick W. Axelgard, ed., *Iraq in Transition: A Political, Economic and Strategic Perspective*. Boulder, CO: Westview, 1986.

Darwish, Abel and Gregory Alexander. *Unholy Babylon*. London: Victor Gollancz Ltd., 1991.

Dawisha, Adeed. "The Politics of War: Presidential Centrality, Party Power, Political Opposition" in Frederick W. Axelgard, ed., *Iraq in Transition: A Political, Economic and Strategic Perspective*. Boulder, CO: Westview, 1986.

Evans, Michael. *The Gulf Crisis*. London: Franklin Watts, 1988.

Farouk-Sluglett, Marion and Peter Sluglett. *Iraq Since 1958: From Revolution to Dictatorship*. London: KPI, 1987.

Gardner, J. Anthony. *The Iran-Iraq War: A Bibliography*. London: Mansell, 1988.

Gera, Gideon. "Iraq's Strategy--Towards Regional Dominance," *Middle East Focus*, vol. 13, no. 1, Spring 1991.

Ghareeb, Edmund. "Iraq in the Gulf," in Frederick W. Axelgard, ed., *Iraq in Transition: A Political, Economic and Strategic Perspective*. Boulder, CO: Westview, 1986.

Ghareeb, Edmund. *The Kurdish Question in Iraq*. New York: Syracuse University Press, 1981.

Goldschmidt, Arthur, Jr. *A Concise History of the Middle East*, 3d ed. Boulder, CO: Westview, 1988.

Halliday, Fred. "Biting the Western Hand That Helped Them," *Manchester Guardian Weekly*, August 19, 1990.

Halliday, Fred. "Iran-Iraq: The Uncertainties of Peace," *World Today*, vol. 44, October 1988.

Halpern, Manfred. *The Politics of Social Change in the Middle East and North Africa*. Princeton, N. J.: Princeton University Press, 1963.

Hamadi, Sa'adun. "Some Aspects of Economic Policy in Iraq in the Post-War Period" (Arabic text). A speech delivered at the Annual Banquet for Iraqis in the United Kingdom, January 25, 1989.

Hameed, Mazher. *Saudi Arabia, the West and the Security of the Gulf*. London: Croom Helm, 1986.

Heller, Mark A. *The Iran-Iraq War: Implications for Third Countries*. Jaffee Center for Strategic Studies. Paper no. 23. Tel Aviv: Jaffee Center for

Strategic Studies, 1984.

Heller, Mark A., Dov Tamari and Zeev Eytan, eds. *The Middle East Military Balance, 1983*. Tel Aviv: Tel Aviv University, 1983.

Heller, Mark A., Dov Tamari and Zeev Eytan, eds. *The Middle East Military Balance, 1984*. Tel Aviv: Tel Aviv University, 1983.

Hussein, Saddam. *On Gulf War*. Baghdad: Dar al-Mamun, 1988.

Hussein, Saddam. *Saddam Hussein on the Conflict with Iran*. London: Embassy of the Republic of Iraq--Press Office, 1980.

Jansen, G. H. *Militant Islam*. London: Pan Books, 1979.

Jawad, Sa'ad. *Iraq and the Kurdish Question, 1958-1970*. London: Ithaca Press, 1981.

Karsh, Efraim, ed. *The Iran-Iraq War: Impact and Implications*. Tel Aviv: Jaffee Center for Strategic Studies, 1987.

Karsh, Efraim and P. Rautsi. *Saddam Hussein: A Political Biography*. New York: Free Press, 1991.

Lewis, Bernard. "The Return of Islam," Michael Curtis, ed., *Religion and Politics in the Middle East*. Boulder, CO: Westview, 1981.

Long, David E. "Islamic Republic of Iran," David E. Long and Bernard Reich, eds., *The Government and Politics of the Middle East and North Africa*, 2d ed. Boulder: Westview, 1986.

McKinnon, Dan. *Bullseye Iraq*. New York: Berkley Books, 1987.

Mansfield, Peter. "Saddam Husain's Political Thinking: The Comparison with Nasser," Tim Niblock, ed. *Iraq: The Contemporary State*. London: Croom Helm, 1982.

Marr, Phebe. *The Modern History of Iraq*. Boulder, CO: Westview, 1985.

Matar, Fouad. *Saddam Hussein: A Biography*. London: Highlight Productions, 1990.

Matar, Fuad. *Saddam Hussein: The Man, the Cause and the Future*. London: Third World Centre, 1981.

Mendelsohn, Everett. "The End of the Cold War: Implications for Israeli-Palestinian Peace Making." A paper prepared for the Seminar on U.S. Foreign Policy in the Middle East, May 5-6, 1990. Amman, Jordan: Arab Thought Forum, 1990.

Miller, Judith and Laurie Mylroie. *Saddam Hussein and the Crisis in the Gulf.* New York: Times Books, 1990.

Morris, Captain M. E. *H. Norman Schwarzkopf: Road to Triumph.* New York: St. Martin's Press, 1991.

Mortimer, Edward. "The Thief of Baghdad," *New York Review*, September 27, 1990.

Mosalem, Talaat Ahmed. "The Military Bases and Foreign Military Presence. A Threat to Red Sea and Indian Ocean Security." Paper submitted to the International Conference on Peace, Security and Cooperation in the Red Sea, Arab Gulf and Indian Ocean. Aden, January 19-21, 1990.

Mottale, Morris M. "The Other War," *Middle East Focus*, March 1983.

O'Ballance, Edgar. *The Gulf War.* London: Brassey's, 1988.

Patai, Raphael. *The Arab Mind*, revised ed. New York: Charles Scribner's and Sons, 1983.

Pelletiere, Stephen C. *The Kurds: An Unstable Element in the Gulf.* Boulder, CO: Westview, 1984.

Pelletiere, Stephen C. *The Kurds and Their Agas: An Assessment of the Situation in Northern Iraq.* Carlisle Barracks, Penn.: Strategic Studies Institute, U.S. Army War College, 1991.

Pelletiere, Stephen C., Douglas V. Johnson II, and Leif R. Rosenberger. *Iraqi Power and U.S. Security in the Middle East.* Carlisle Barracks, Penn.: Strategic Studies Institute, U.S. Army War College, 1990.

Rezun, Miron, ed. *Iran at the Crossroads: Global Relations in a Turbulent Decade.* Boulder, CO: Westview, 1990.

Salinger, Pierre and Eric Laurent. *Secret Dossier: The Hidden Agenda Behind the Gulf War.* Trans. from the French by Howard Curtis. New York: Penguin, 1991.

Sasson, Jean P. *The Rape of Kuwait.* New York: Knightsbridge, 1991.

Sigler, John. "The Legacy of the Iran-Iraq War," Miron Rezun, ed., *Iran at the Crossroads: Global Relations in a Turbulent Decade.* Boulder, CO: Westview, 1990.

Smith, Hedrick. *The Power Game: How Washington Works.* New York: Ballantine, 1988.

Smith, Wilfred Cantwell. "Understanding Islam," *The Illustrated Encyclo pedia Yearbook*, 1981.

Truth About Kurds in Iraq, The. London: Embassy of the Republic of Iraq-- Press Office, July 1989.

Tumas, Elias H. "The Gulf Crisis: Still There Are Ways Out Of It," *Middle East Focus*, vol. 13, no. 1, Spring 1991.

Tyler, Patrick E. "Could Iraq Survive as a Nation Without Saddam?," *Manchester Guardian Weekly*, October 14, 1990.

Walker, Martin. "A Buffalo Soldier on the Brink," *Manchester Guardian Weekly*, February 24, 1991.

Woodward, Bob. *The Commanders.* New York: Simon and Schuster, 1991.

NEWSPAPERS

Al-Ahram, Cairo.

Al-Jazeira, Riyadh, Saudi Arabia.

Al-Khalij Al-'Arabi, Saudi Arabia.

Al-Sharq Al-Awsat, London.

Al-Thawrah, Baghdad.

Al-Wafd, Cairo.

Dirasaat al-Khaleej wal Jazeera al-'Arabiyya.

Economist, Quarterly Energy Review--Middle East, 1981-1990, London.

Guardian, London.

Ha'Aretz, Tel Aviv.

Jane's Defense Weekly, London.

Kaihan International, Teheran.

Le Monde, Paris.

Majallat Al-'Amal, Amman, Jordan.

The New York Times.

Yediot Aharonot, Tel Aviv.

Index

ABOUT THE AUTHOR

MIRON REZUN currently lives and teaches in Canada, where he is Professor of Political Science at the University of New Brunswick. A native of Israel, he studied in Geneva, Switzerland, after serving in the Israeli military. He was then a war correspondent based in Switzerland and France before being detached to Afghanistan and the Middle East. Miron Rezun has traveled many times to the Soviet Union and to Soviet Central Asia, as well as to Iran and Turkey, publishing extensively on Soviet and Mideastern affairs. His most recent titles are *Intrigue and War in Southwest Asia* (Praeger, 1991) and *Post-Khomeini Iran and the New Gulf War* (1992). He has also edited the forthcoming *Nationalism and the Breakup of Empire* (Praeger, 1992) and *Iran at the Crossroads* (1990). His present project is "Nationalism and Ethnicity in Yugoslavia: European Dimensions," co-authored with Sava Bosnitch.